Dan Rice, D.V.M.

Bengal Cats

Everything About Purchase, Care,
Nutrition, Health Care, and Behavior

Filled with Full-Color Photographs
Illustrations by Michele Earle-Bridges

D0565035

BARRON'S

²CONTENTS

3 2113 00774 1427

Breeding Complexities   69
Profitability Issues   70

Health Care   73

Hybrid Vigor   73
Vaccines   73
Infectious Diseases   76
Skin Diseases   81
Internal Parasites   82
Hormonal Imbalances   83
Poisoning (Toxicosis)   83
Metabolic Diseases of
Older Cats   86

Congenital Deformities   86
Giving Your Bengal a Pill   87
Symptoms of Illnesses   90
Euthanasia   91

Information   92

Index   94

INTRODUCTION TO THE BENGAL

No doubt all domestic breeds of cats can trace their origin to feral ancestors. Certainly small, wild cats that closely resemble the common house cat can be found throughout much of the eastern world. One principal difference between all other domestic cats and the Bengal is its proximity to its wild ancestor.

Bengals always seem to be posing.

Bengal Ancestry

The Bengal cat of this book is a domesticated house cat. It is an even-tempered, gentle, affectionate, and playful family pet. The name of the breed, Bengal, has no relationship to the Bengal tiger.

The domestic Bengal derived its name from the species name of its wild ancestor, *Felis bengalensis,* an Asian leopard cat. The Bengal cat that is discussed in detail in the following chapters is four or more generations removed from that wild species. Its appearance is similar to the Asian leopard cat, and its genetic makeup contains a contribution from that wild cat species. *Its temperament, however, is purely domestic.* The purposeful production of a domestic breed from a wild species was a

difficult and time-consuming task. The goal in developing the domestic Bengal cat breed was to preserve a strong physical resemblance to its beautiful wild ancestor. At the same time, the new domestic breed was designed to be a pleasant and trustworthy family companion.

Production of the Bengal breed required diluting and virtually eliminating the timid, reclusive, and untamable characteristics inherent in the wild leopard cat species. That genetic dilution has been done by experts who have carefully crossbred the Asian leopard cat with certain domestic cats. As with any new breed of cats, a great deal of curiosity exists about the Bengal. The questions most frequently asked relate to the breed characteristics, and to the authenticity of its wild origin. Naturally, many prospective Bengal owners want to know more about the breed's ancestral wild Asian leopard cat.

Classification of the Asian Leopard Cat
ORDER: **Carnivora**
   FAMILY: **Felidae**
      GENUS: *Acinonyx*   (cheetah)
               Panthera   (lion, tiger, leopard)
               Felis   (house cat, leopard cat, golden cat, ocelot, margay, lynx, caracal, mountain lion, jaguarundi, pampas cat, Andean cat, Palla's cat, clouded leopard, marbled cat, serval, fishing cat, flat-headed cat)

Description of the Asian Leopard Cat

Asian leopard cats are wild animals with many of the traits of other wild felines. Like other wild animals, leopard cats' instinctive, genetically wired traits surface as they mature. A newborn Asian leopard kitten that is taken from its dam at birth, nursed by a domestic cat, and handled daily by a human, may temporarily appear to bond to its human counterpart. It may accept handling, petting, and playing with humans for several months; then it grows up.

No matter how Asian leopard cats are raised, when sexually mature, they are not tame or domesticated. They don't spend the evening purring contentedly on your lap. They are solitary, nocturnal, wild animals that are shy and reclusive, and will rarely allow handling or touching by a human. They instinctively resent being "cornered," and may become aggressively defensive when protecting their young. Like other wild animals, they usually have no interest in human companionship, and receive no pleasure from petting.

Like most wild felines, they will adapt to zoolike surroundings, where they can hide or pace, depending on their moods. They will spray urine on walls and bedding, defecate from high perches, and urinate or defecate in their drinking water. Observers and students of this species agree that although the leopard cat is small in size by comparison to the tiger, lion, leopard, and cougar, it is probably less tamable.

The leopard cats' habitat extends throughout Asia, including the mainland and the island countries. Some of the leopard cat varieties have their own descriptive names that are related to the particular region or country in which they occur. Other subspecies have common names that describe their habits, such as "the fishing cat." Physically descriptive common names such as "rusty spotted cat" or "flat-headed cat" are used to identify other subspecies. In some regions of Asia, leopard cats are nearly extinct, and many species are considered endangered or threatened.

Coat Characteristics

The intensity of coat colors of Asian leopard cats are darkest in the warmer regions and lightest in the cool climates of the continent. Background coat colors vary from light, hazy blue-gray or tan to dark brown or dark gray, with shades of yellow and green occurring in some. All share the horizontally aligned or random contrasting spots that are characteristic of the species. Some have spots that resemble rosettes, whereas others have solid colored spots. Some have triangular shaped spots, others are round. The ocelli, which is a very noticeable white spot on the back of their dark colored ears, is common to all leopard cats. Black spots above the eyes, black tail tip, spotted, light-colored bellies, and black and white stripes on their faces are also prevalent markings.

The general body structure of *Felis bengalensis* is similar to that of domestic felines. Some subspecies are a bit larger, some smaller, ranging in weight from 10 to 15 pounds (4.5–6.8 kg). Characteristics generally applicable to all are wedge-shaped heads and prominent eyes. They have small, rounded ears, and their hindquarters are heavily muscled, with hind legs proportionately longer than those of domestic cats.

Asian leopard cats are expert swimmers and very active climbers. In spite of their diminutive size, they are very effective, cunning, nocturnal hunters. They inhabit forests, jungles, brush country, and plains, and are usually found near water. Among their natural prey are rodents, bats, birds, fish, and occasionally young hoofed animals larger than themselves.

History of the Bengal Breed

Bengals are among the newest breeds to be developed, and have only recently been added to the list of domestic cat breeds. They join the older, more populous breeds such as Siamese, Burmese, Abyssinian, Persian, and other house cats. The Bengal's history and its unique and lovely leopardlike appearance set it clearly apart from other domestic breeds, but, like them, it was developed as a family pet. According to The International Cat Association (TICA), Bengal cat registrations were 41,507 in 2002, and this number continues to grow by approximately 10 percent per year.

In the United States, the first intentional and controlled hybridization of a domestic cat with the wild Asian leopard cat by Jean Sugden Mill was recorded in 1965 in Arizona.

Other breeding was done in the 1970s and the name Bengal was adopted as the official breed name, but the bloodlines originating during that period were not perpetuated. Early in the 1980s, Ms. Mill joined forces with other Bengal enthusiasts and started two different bloodlines. Through their efforts, breed standards were established and registration was undertaken by TICA.

By 1984, Bengal cats from a number of bloodlines were exhibited and judged in TICA shows worldwide in the New Breed and Color class.

The Bengal's Wild Ancestry

Asian leopard cats were co-progenitors of all Bengals, and their current gene pool includes a significant contribution from the wild *Felis bengalensis,* from which the Bengal's name is derived. The percentage of wild blood in a domestic Bengal is irrelevant. It may not even be possible to calculate that percentage accurately. More important is the breed standard that specifies that Bengals must have physical features distinctive to the small forest-dwelling wild cats. Special merit is given to those animals that have an appearance that

Bengal Competition
In 1990, Bengals were accepted by TICA for championship competition in their shows. The Bengal is now an authentic domestic cat breed, in spite of its rather recent development.

A typical adult female Bengal with oodles of spots.

Female wild Asian leopard cat Arvay Ritz of Rosettea.

above: Athletic Bengal in a tree.

above right: Have a look at my back side.

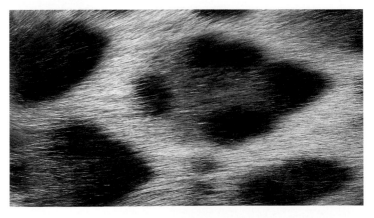

A close-up of a perfect rosette.

sets them distinctly apart from other domestic cat breeds.

Today's breeders strive to produce Bengals that possess predictable housecat personalities and temperaments. The best Bengals mimic the conformation, color, size, and coat patterns of the wild Asian leopard cat but not its fierce, feral personality. For obvious reasons, owners, veterinarians, show judges, and others who have reason to handle cats must be assured that Bengals who occupy our homes and those who are seen in shows and on exam tables are not wild cats but docile, domestic companion cats.

Pedigree records are kept by TICA on all Bengals, even those that cannot compete in shows. The foundation stock of Bengals that are registered in an experimental category includes Asian leopard cats and the first three generations of outcrosses. In order to register an Asian leopard cat, TICA requires pictures and detailed information relative to the ownership, origin, and location of the animal.

The Bengal's Domestic Ancestors

The Egyptian Mau is a domestic cat breed with a desirable temperament, whose spotted coat patterns breed true from generation to generation. Those and possibly other considerations made the Mau, especially the Indian variety, one of the several domestic breeds chosen to be used as domestic foundation stock that produced Bengals. Other breeds, such as the Abyssinian, Burmese, and various domestic tabby cats were used as well.

In the first (F-1) generation, the coat color and patterns of Asian leopard cats tend to dominate those of domestic cats used in the outcross. In the following generations, however, the diverse genes from the domestic cats, especially those of mixed breeds, make the selection of domestic foundation breeding stock a challenge. Only fourth generation and beyond can be considered domestic Bengals in every sense of the word.

Hybridization

The first generation Bengal cats were, by definition, hybrids. That is to say, their parents were from two different species.

The hybrid offspring of the mating of those two different species is referred to as the F-1 generation. Males of the first (F-1) generation are sterile. Therefore, in the development of Bengals, an F-1 female was bred to a domestic cat, producing the second (F-2) generation of kittens. Second generation females were bred to Bengals or other domestic cats to produce the third (F-3) generation. Sterility is observed in males of the F-2 and F-3 generations as well. Animals in those three foundation stock generations (F-1, F-2, and F-3) are not eligible for championship showing as Bengals. Together with the Asian leopard cat, they are registered by TICA in the experimental category.

Registry and Competition Problems

The unique genetic composition of Bengals is not all good news, however. It prevents the breed's recognition by some cat registries. It eliminates them from registration and championship competition in the shows of most cat organizations, whose rules do not allow cats with wild blood to be exhibited, irrespective of the character or disposition of the cat.

Bengals of the F-4 generation and beyond are uniformly acceptable as family pets. The breeders of Bengals select their propagation stock according to each animal's conformity to breed standards, including disposition and physical characteristics, irrespective of their percentage of wild blood.

Survival of Felis Catus

Bengal cats aren't just another example of spotted alley cats that have garnered a fancy new name. However, these beautiful creatures belong in homes, not in Dumpsters. They have enjoyed an illustrious beginning that deserves preservation much like our forest wildlife. Cats are survivors, and Bengal cats are simply creatures that have been purposefully domesticated from the wild by dilution, then through careful selective breeding. This process has caused certain changes in their phenotype and genotype that set them aside from other breeds.

Given half a chance, any domestic cat will hold its own on the streets and alleys of the cities and back roads of rural communities. All cats have built-in survival mechanisms that give them the ability to hunt their natural prey. If prey is not available, they will scrounge through trash bins. They can reproduce in barns, sheds, or even on the rooftops of high rises. Domestic cats may join cockroaches and coyotes and become one of the last species to survive on Earth.

If you are sufficiently fortunate to acquire a Bengal, treasure it, enjoy its unique habits, and appreciate its beautiful colors and personality. However, if for any reason you can't keep it, don't sell it to the highest bidder. That might promote indiscriminate breeding or even abuse. Don't turn it outdoors if your new landlord won't allow you to keep a pet. Don't give it up to the children down the block who need a cat. Instead, contact the breeder from whom you bought the Bengal and if she isn't interested in reclaiming and rehoming it, contact one of the national Bengal clubs. Bengal rescues are quickly forming as the breed's popularity grows. The fanciers and breeders know the Bengal well and understand its needs and will surely help you find a perfect home for it.

UNDERSTANDING BENGAL CATS

Bengals are delightfully safe pets to own. They easily meet the breed standards that require loving, dependable temperaments.

Although individual Bengals, like any other breed, may be less desirable than others, the potential for their reversion to the disposition of their feral ancestors is remote.

The disposition of Bengals is comparable to that of many other domestic cat breeds. Typically, they are outgoing, curious, playful, and affectionate pets. They are rarely timid or reclusive and they easily blend into the social order of their family and bond to its members. Bengals enjoy gentle handling and grooming by adults and children alike. They are happy, responsive souls that possess exceptional intelligence and trainability.

Comments frequently heard from Bengal owners dwell on their inherent mental keenness. Some believe that the breed has a skull size that is proportionally larger than other domestic breeds, and suggest that may be associated with greater brain mass and capacity.

Bengals are not vocal cats that pester their owners, wanting to give their opinions on every subject, but they will converse when

Note the spots on Cisco's white belly.

given the opportunity and when encouraged to do so. An interesting short, rather guttural barking sound is sometimes heard from Bengals, especially when fed some particularly tasty treat.

The Aquatic Bengal

Bengals are reputed to have an affinity for water. Many will take an uninvited dip in the bathtub with their owners, and others have a propensity to share the shower or lavatory with their human companions. Bengal kittens frequently play in their water bowls, and their toys are often found floating about in their dishes. No data is available relative to Bengals' habits around household fish tanks, but it may be wise to cover your tanks if they are within reach of an adventuresome Bengal.

The Climbing Bengal

Another Bengal peculiarity is its affinity for height. Breeding kennels are usually fitted out with platforms near the ceiling, where the resident Bengal is frequently found in regal posture, surveying its estate. Bengals are accomplished climbers, and spend a good deal of time in trees or on high climbing posts when available. Bengals are very surefooted creatures with extraordinary athletic abilities that would be expected in cats with their heritage.

They are busy pets that enjoy exercise, and most will use large running wheels similar to the small ones found in hamster cages. Their sleek, trim, athletic conformation and solid musculature is enhanced by their instinctive climbing and running exercises.

Bengals are very positive, independent animals, not at all shy or withdrawn. They freely accept other animals, but they are not likely to be found at the bottom of the pecking order of the household pets. They commonly share their space on an equal basis with other breeds of cats and with dogs. They are not fragile or timid, neither are they contrary nor aggressive.

Handling a Bengal is like handling any other cat. If treated gently when young, a kitten will grow up to be a gentle cat. If a cat of any breed is treated roughly, abused, or frightened consistently, it will become reclusive, defensive, and resentful.

Appearance

A handsome Bengal's coat should be soft and smooth like a pelt. There are two coat patterns recognized, spotted and marbled.

The popular spotted pattern closely resembles the Asian leopard cat's appearance. Spotted Bengals have dark spots on a contrasting lighter background color. The spots take various shapes and are arranged in a horizontal alignment over the body, or sometimes in a random configuration. That differs from the vertical spotting patterns and stripes found on tabbies and other breeds.

Rosettes

Rosette spots, common to the wild leopard cats, have multishaded light centers or shadows on the dark spots. Rosettes are quite striking in appearance, and are very desirable. Bengals are the only domestic purebreds that possess rosettes, and the genetics of their transmission is still being worked out by Bengal breeders.

Marbling

The marbled pattern is uniquely different from the spotted pattern, and it also has great eye appeal. Although wild felines such as the clouded leopard demonstrate marbling, Asian leopard cats in the Bengal ancestry are not known to possess that coat pattern. Marbled Bengals are believed to result from domestic butterfly tabbies that were used in early development of Bengals. The multishade, horizontally aligned rosettes of Asian leopard cats somehow influence the marbling characteristic, resulting in the Bengal's horizontally flowing marble patterns.

Marbled Bengals' dark whorls on a lighter background should have several distinctive outlines of slightly darker colors.

The desired marble pattern has a random horizontal flow on the side of the cat that is distinctly different from the bull's-eye patterns in butterfly tabby cats. Vertical stripes, commonly seen in mackerel tabbies, are undesirable in Bengals. Bengal color and pattern genetics are complex.

There are presently three Bengal colors recognized:

1. the brown tabby
2. the seal lynx point
3. the seal sepia tabby/seal mink tabby.

(Other colors—silver, blue, and solid black—are being accepted for evaluation competition in the New Breed and Color class.)

All Bengals should have black or nearly black tips on their tails, and light-colored, spotted bellies. Bengals weigh up to about 15 pounds (6.8 kg) and have small, rounded ears and a slightly Roman nose. Many Bengals have prominent white tactile whisker pads on their muzzles that are very distinctive. Bengals have trim, well-knit, powerful bodies, similar to those of Asian leopard cats.

Pets Versus Show Cats

A Bengal is a Bengal is a Bengal. Right? Wrong! A pet-quality Bengal differs from a show-quality cat, which differs from a breeding-quality animal. All three may meet the minimum standards for the breed, but purchase prices will vary greatly. There should, however, be no difference between the personalities of the various qualities of Bengals. A fancy show-winning Bengal's disposition should be just as desirable as that of a pet-quality cat, and vice versa.

Breeders who are now propagating the many different Bengal bloodlines are naturally developing minute differences in the appearance of their cats that tend to identify their own lines. They study the individuals that possess the various desirable characteristics, and through careful selection of breeding stock, they strengthen and fix those features in their bloodlines.

The acceptable variations in physical conformation, coat, and color may be more or less desirable, depending on the purpose for which the cat is acquired. Before purchasing a Bengal for showing or breeding purposes, the breed standard should be memorized. At the same time, winning Bengals in the show rings should be studied to establish a personal knowledge of the best of the breed.

Pet Qualities

If acquisition of a pet Bengal is the goal, selection should be made according to the appeal of an animal to the buyer. Consideration should always be given to the breed standard and the conformity of the cat to that standard, but the eye appeal, personality, and health of a pet are equally important.

Show-quality faults may be easily overlooked by a pet buyer if a kitten is particularly winsome, affectionate, active, and healthy. Pet cats should be castrated or spayed at or before maturity, and many pet-quality kittens are sold without registration papers. You may want your Bengal to look like other Bengals, but rigid compliance with all the standards applied to show cats does not increase the companion value of a pet Bengal.

BENGAL OWNERSHIP

There are many factors to consider before you decide upon the addition of a Bengal or any other cat to your household. First, you must love cats.

A Bengal cat requires about the same care as cats of other breeds. It is not encumbered with a finicky appetite or objectionable habits. It is easily litter box trained and can be kept in your home all its life with little special attention.

For the Love of Cats

Cat lovers are found in all walks of life, and in every conceivable circumstance. They are the fortunate individuals who have come to appreciate cats as housemates. Many people are hooked into ownership of a cat under false pretenses. They hear about the independence and undemanding character of cats as pets, and they believe it!

A few weeks later their homes are arrayed with a dozen pieces of cat furniture, and their pantry shelves are stocked with a variety of cat foods and treats. Their lives are wonderfully enriched by the presence of a royal dignitary with a name like Sweetcakes. They clean litter

Just what I need, a feather duster.

boxes, sleep with furry tails in their faces, and awake to the tune of loud feline motors— all for the honor of sharing their lives with 10 pounds (4.5 kg) of fur and purr.

They resent any suggestion that they have some deep attachment to their cats, and they swear that when Sweetcakes is gone, they will never have another pet. Deep inside, however, the thought of being without a cat in the family is untenable. Within the ranks of cat lovers are those who are attached to specific breeds of cats. They have discovered that individuals of certain breeds are more interesting and have more charisma and charm than others.

Why Own a Bengal?

Bengal cats combine many of the majestic physical features of Asian leopard cats with the lovable personalities of domestic house cats. Their appearance is startling at first, and will be the topic of conversations with your friends.

If you are fascinated by rare and unique personalities, you will undoubtedly enjoy the companionship of a Bengal. If you appreciate the unusual, a Bengal pet may be an excellent choice for you. Don't be surprised the first time your Bengal joins you in the bathtub, or when you first discover it lying in royal posture, surveying its kingdom from some almost inaccessibly high vantage point.

Bengals typically are not aggressive pets, but if you expect to find an inanimate couch potato clad in the beautiful colors and patterns of a Bengal, you will be disappointed. As in other breeds, each animal is endowed with its own personality.

Cost of a Bengal

There is no such thing as a free pet. Even a kitten that is taken in as a refugee from a storm, or is found on your doorstep, has costs associated with its care. The Bengal kitten that you choose to share your home and life will be your companion for a very long time. Cats often live to ripe old ages, many as long as 15 or 18 years. The initial cost of purchase reflects the magnitude of your desire to have a particular Bengal cat. However, the financial obligations associated with the day by day ownership of a Bengal are no greater than those associated with ownership of a free tabby. Costs are offset by hundreds of joyful hours that a feline companion will bring to your life. Cat lovers

receive daily rewards for the time and money they invest in their pets.

Price Variations

You can expect to pay for the rarity of a Bengal. The purchase cost depends upon many factors. If you are shopping for an animal with very few breed faults and one that will hold its own in championship showing, you are probably looking at a price of $1,000 to $3,000 or more. Prices in the same range or slightly higher are charged for breeding stock, because only the best animals are used to perpetuate the breed, and many breeding-quality animals have cat show titles.

Pet Bengals are a bit easier on the purse. Depending upon the quality of the individual, Bengal kittens that are sold as pets range in price from $200 to $500. Some may be sold for less if they have significant undesirable flaws in their conformation, color, or coat patterns. On occasion, some pet Bengal kittens are even given away to good homes by a breeder. You should expect strict requirements attached to a pet kitten. Some breeders will only part with them if the new owner guarantees that the pet will be confined to your home and altered at maturity.

Status Symbols

Sometimes exotic cats are purchased to impress friends and neighbors and not because they are fascinating, interesting, and beautiful pets. This is true of all somewhat expensive or rare cats and is especially so in the case of Bengals.

You may decide that a Bengal will bring a mysterious flare to its environment, add fascinating colors to its surroundings, and can be used as window decoration in an otherwise drab household. Owning a Bengal might be considered the *in* thing to do. Like any other valuable possession it might serve to elevate you to a step above the commonplace *cat* owner. That plan will ensnare you and trap an otherwise fine pet into a horrible life.

Please don't use the same motive for your Bengal purchase as you would for inanimate objects. A Bengal is a living, purring, playful living being. You can't keep it locked up in a closet and take it out for company on weekends. It will be an active participant in family gatherings. It won't accept being a centerpiece for your living room décor.

Bengals sometimes display a regal demeanor and act like royalty but a kitten is a mischievous little critter whether it originated in a fancy cattery from pedigreed parents or in a back alley trash Dumpster. Today's Bengal is a domestic cat in a beautiful coat. It looks different because of its startling markings, its long hind legs, and its rounded ears but in the final analysis, it's a domestic feline. It has retained some of its ancestral habits such as climbing perches, daily exercise, and playing in water but in spite of or because of these interesting characteristics, it deserves an active place in your family, not a shelf upon which to be displayed.

In order to grow up as an honored member of your family, a Bengal kitten must be properly trained and taught its place in the home. It will climb your curtains if allowed to do so and catch the fish from your aquarium if you don't cover the tank. It will use your best bedspread or Turkish rug as scratching mats if you don't nip that habit in the bud. A Bengal may be highly protective of its food and this point should be blunted with proper training. Without appropriate training, a Bengal kitten will beg and cry for food at your table and if you're not watching closely it will snatch a favored tidbit right from your fork.

Don't fall into the status symbol trap. Purchase a Bengal only after you have discussed its training with your family and only after you are certain of your motives.

Food and Health Care Costs

The costs of food and veterinary service for a Bengal are no different from those incurred for any other cat. If you are planning to cut the costs of ownership by buying the cheapest brand of food for your Bengal, or ignoring its health care, you may be disappointed in the results. The costs of food and litter are nominal. Like health care, those ongoing costs are a necessary part of pet ownership.

GETTING READY FOR YOUR BENGAL KITTEN

Before you bring a Bengal, or any cat for that matter, into your home, be sure that you understand the obligation you are taking upon yourself.

The first consideration when deciding to buy a Bengal is your ability and desire to take care of the new pet. Are you willing and able to provide for it for the next ten or 15 years? That is a question sometimes ignored by prospective pet owners.

For its safety, your Bengal should be confined to your home day and night. To do otherwise is to contribute to the already overwhelming problem of stray and abandoned cats. Cats that are allowed out of the house, even briefly, often meet with disaster.

Cat Furniture

Certain items are needed by your new companion. Its bed need be nothing more than a small cardboard box with an old towel or sweater for bedding. Bengals love heights, so if

So many toys, so little time.

you purchase a cat condominium, choose one with a high observation platform.

Litter Box

A litter box is another essential. Any impermeable, flat-bottomed container will work. It should have sides at least 4 or 6 inches (10–15.2 cm) tall to contain the litter. Manufactured litter boxes are available in pet supply stores. Some come equipped with covers, swinging doors, and deodorant dispensers.

Litter Material

Commercial litter is made of small clay particles that are very absorptive, facilitating the litter box cleaning process. Litter cost depends on the packaging, the deodorants used, and the brand names. To find the one that works best for you, experiment with different litter products, using a small bag of one, then another.

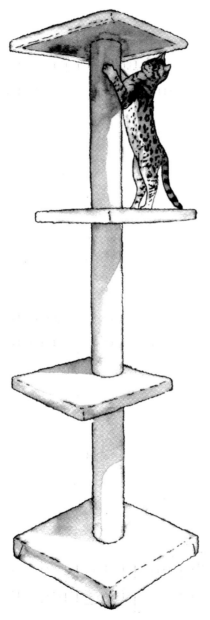

Cat tower.

Some litter material has a propensity to stick to the hair of a cat's feet and fall onto the carpet. Others have perfumes that are objectionable to cats. Some products cause urine to clump, making cleaning easier. (If ingested, clumping litter can cause severe problems in kittens, and its use is not recommended for them.) Litter pan liners are plastic bags that can be used inside a litter pan to facilitate dumping the litter and excrement easily, with less mess.

Hiding Places

A place of refuge is another must, especially if there are children or other pets in the family. Every cat, no matter what its age, needs a place to go when it wants to be left alone for a nap. A cardboard box about 12 or 14 inches (30.5–35.6 cm) square, with a top on it, works fine for that purpose. Cut a hole in one end, just large enough to allow the kitten to enter. Put an old towel or some article of your clothing in the box, and place it in a secluded place.

The top platform of a cat condo is a favorite refuge for adult Bengals. Any cozy location that is inaccessible to other pets is acceptable. It is important that all members of the family honor your Bengal's place of refuge.

Scratching Posts

The outer layers of cats' retractable claws flake off normally. All cats extend their claws and scratch on something to facilitate that normal flaking. Soft bark of young trees is one of the preferred natural materials for working their nails. Because most homes don't have trees growing in them, your indoor Bengal will probably use a chair or sofa. Due to the cost of reupholstering

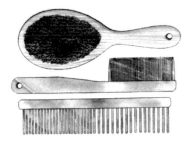

Essential grooming tools: comb, flea comb, and brush.

Food and Water Dishes

The safest vessels to use are stainless steel food and water dishes that are available in pet supply stores. Some ceramic dishes have been reported to release paint or firing chemicals when water is kept in them continuously. Some plastics may also release chemicals into the water after it has been kept in the dish for a long period of time.

The Security of Confinement

A culture shock must be expected when a kitten is taken from its mother, the security of its nursery, and the companionship of its littermates. The trauma of changing environments can be minimized by confinement of the newcomer for a few days when it arrives in your home. That is especially important if there are children or other pets in the house, or if

furniture, that habit is rarely acceptable, so it is best to have a scratching post in place when you bring the kitten home. You can make such a post out of a short section of soft wood, or you can buy a fancy commercial model, covered with carpet or sisal rope. Although the manufactured models cost more than a piece of wood nailed to a platform, they last for years.

Some cats prefer to work their claws on carpet. In that case, provide a swatch of discarded carpet material about 18 inches (45.7 cm) square. Lay the carpet swatch on the floor upside down, so your Bengal can work its claws into the jute backing.

Grooming Tools

A brush and a fine comb, manufactured specifically for cats, should be purchased. If fleas are indigenous to your area, a very fine-tooth flea comb will help to identify those parasites on your Bengal.

Nail trimmers of various designs are available, but, the best ones are those that cut the nail cleanly with no crushing effect that causes pain to your pet. Because nails should be trimmed every couple of weeks, be sure that you make the procedure as quick and painless as possible.

Variety of cat furnishings.

I'll get that pesky little
varmint next time.

Stretching to show a
terrifically spotted tummy.

Is that thing loaded?

Curious Bengal investigating a bug.

A Bengal walking on a leash.

Grooming Avalanche is no chore.

the adults are gone from the house during the day. Confinement in a bathroom works well, but any small room that you can temporarily rig as a halfway house will do. The less furniture in the room, the better. If it is impossible to appropriate a small confinement room for a week or so, consider the purchase of a large wire kennel from a pet supply store.

Boarding Your Pet

If you plan to be gone from home occasionally, you should plan in advance for your Bengal's care during your absence. A clean, well-recommended cat boarding facility may be chosen, but better yet is a friend who will stop in at your home every day to check on your cat. Cats are happier and at less risk of accident or illness in their own homes. If someone can be found who will clean the litter box regularly and provide fresh water and food daily, that is ideal. Another possibility to consider is a friend who will take the Bengal into her or his home and provide for it there.

Medical Services

Health care is of extreme importance. Bengals are notoriously hardy cats, but accidents and illnesses occur, even in the most careful families. If you do not already have a professional relationship with a local veterinarian, establish one before bringing your kitten home. You can sometimes find one who has special expertise or training in cat health, but most companion animal clinicians have adequate interest and knowledge of feline medicine and surgery. There are a number of subjects that should be discussed with your veterinarian.

✔ a preventive health care plan for the kitten, including vaccination and physical examination schedules
✔ the possibility of health insurance
✔ subscription to a pet health newsletter
✔ dietary advice, including vitamin supplementation
✔ the availability of emergency care

If possible, make an appointment to meet the veterinarian and discuss those topics before you acquire your kitten. Then take the kitten to the veterinarian before you take it home. A brief physical examination may reveal some obscure problem. If such a problem is discovered immediately and you don't want to deal with it, the breeder will likely agree to replace the kitten. Although that thought may be very distasteful to you, it is far better to deal with problems as soon as they are discovered, before the inevitable attachment has joined you and your Bengal.

Prepare Children

Having a new kitten requires everyone to join in the fun. No one can resist the cuddly, purring little body on his lap. Nobody is left out, even if a reluctant family member doesn't particularly like to have a kitten on his pillow every night. You might as well get used to it because Bengals of all ages are clever and quiet when they want to be. One can sneak onto your bed and you won't realize it till you hear her purring loudly right in your ear or feel her fuzzy tail tickling your cheek. Children love kittens as a rule but tiny tots should be instructed not to pick up or carry a kitten because often a kitten will respond to heights by unsheathing its claws and grabbing on for dear life, prompting the child to quickly toss the Bengal to the floor. At 8 or 10 weeks old, a Bengal is fragile and it is subject to injury if dropped.

To the Bengal, nothing is sacred in children's rooms. If it is small enough to be toted about, rolled off the edge, or dragged across the floor, it may be found in a very strange place. Tiny dolls, little trucks, marbles, and any other small object that is discovered on the floor didn't just happen there. The Bengal found them on the dresser top and thought they would look better on the floor.

Kittens love to dart through a door just as it's opened, right under your feet, and they don't need a reason or a plan for that activity either. A wild dash past your foot isn't really to gain entry into another room or go outside. In fact, they might repeat the act in reverse to return to the former place a few minutes later. It is just part of a kitten's job description to try to trip you up. They love to hear what you have to say when you realize that you've nearly squished them into the carpet.

Zooms

Prepare your family for the special experience known to some owners as the crazies or zooms. It may occur anytime during daylight hours or possibly in the middle of the night. Your Bengal kitten is napping or playing with a ball or perhaps trying to catch a fly or bug when suddenly, she jumps in the air and lands running full tilt. She runs from room to room, jumping onto beds, leaping over furniture, careening around corners, and banking off walls. She will slide on tile or hardwood floors, pick up speed on carpets, and dive under sofa pillows and peek out to see if anyone

witnessed her madness. Then as quickly as it began, it's all over. This frenetic activity may last a lifetime, occur every few days, maybe every day for several weeks, or sometimes only occasionally. It's just a typical Bengal burning off excess calories so don't worry.

Try Two

Perhaps your new Bengal is your first cat. You are in for a real treat. Kittens are the most fascinating creatures in the world and Bengals are particularly curious. If you've decided on one Bengal, you might be well advised to get two instead. One Bengal kitten may be all you can afford but if you can find a way, two kittens may be easier to deal with. A single kitten will climb the curtains, push articles from tabletops, hop onto a kitchen counter, and sample the halibut that you just set out for dinner. Just think what it will be like with two! Double the trouble? Maybe not.

Two kittens will keep each other company, and their clever little minds won't be as apt to look for mischief to keep them occupied. They wrestle and chase and entertain you by the hour and still find time to uncover all the popcorn that dropped behind the sofa. If one starts tugging a stray sock across the room, in a heartbeat the pair will devise a game of tug of war. They suddenly collapse in a pile of furry, spotted, bodies and sleep like innocents. They take turns grooming each other, cleaning ears and doing everything except brushing one another's teeth. One will copy the other in nearly every routine of the day. One kitten going into the litter box is followed by the second one, copying the activity. Keep in mind that two will double the work for you when it comes to cleaning the litter box.

SHOPPING FOR YOUR PUREBRED BENGAL

Be very cautious when you purchase a Bengal. Although they may look alike, not all spotted cats are Bengals. Be sure to use a reputable source.

There are many counterfeit Bengals floating around, some with authentic looking pedigrees. Unscrupulous people have been known to purchase a Bengal of pet quality, breed it to a backyard tabby, and advertise the offspring as purebred Bengals.

Sources for Bengals

When you shop for a Bengal from any source, you should first study the breed standards carefully. If possible, visit at least one Bengal cattery and look at their breeding stock as well as the kittens available. Look at the parents and siblings of a kitten before you buy it. Compare those animals with the breed standards and with other Bengal cats in the cattery and ask about perceived differences.

If the seller is unable or unwilling to show you the kitten's parents or some of the kitten's family, and he or she is not well prepared to answer your questions about the kitten, run, don't walk, to the nearest exit.

A spotted desk adornment.

Cat Shows

Try to attend a cat show where you can personally watch the top Bengals of the country in competition for ribbons and titles.

When you attend a cat show, pick up business cards from breeders who have kittens for sale. Bengal breeders who show their cats are the best people to help you begin your kitten search. Information about shows may be obtained from cat associations and clubs and from cat magazines (See Information on page 92).

Newsletters

The next best source of Bengal breeder information is a breed club newsletter (see Bengal Breed Clubs, page 92). Editors of newsletters may send you a free copy. If not, subscription prices are reasonable.

Newspapers

Other sources of Bengal kittens are found in classified ads in newspapers, wherein many ethical breeders advertise their Bengal kittens. Unfortunately, a few disreputable opportunists also advertise in newspapers. That comment is not meant to discourage the potential Bengal owner from contacting breeders who advertise in the paper, only to inspire the prospective buyer's awareness. Ask lots of questions, examine the seller's Bengal knowledge, and look closely at their facilities as well as their kittens and breeding stock.

Kitten Mills

Kitten mills are places (often private homes) that house a collection of registered, purebred cats of both sexes and often of several different breeds. Kitten mill management gives little attention to the breed standards of their animals. Their goal is making money from the sale of mass-produced kittens. Few exhibit their breeding stock in cat shows. The value of cats in a kitten mill lies in their ability to reproduce, not in their conformation or personalities. Kittens thus produced are often marketed through newspaper ads and sometimes through pet shops. The health and quality of Bengals originating in kitten factories are always suspect. It is best to avoid kitten mills as a source of your Bengal.

Mixed Bengals

Be especially wary of ads that offer mixed Bengal kittens, or Bengals without pedigree or registration.

If you should happen to find a healthy spotted kitten that is purported to be a mixed Bengal, and if its appearance and personality strike your fancy, buy it. There is absolutely nothing wrong with a mixed Bengal if it is obtained for the correct reasons. Its value is exactly the same as any other backyard bred cat, and its cost should be the same as that of an average tabby or calico.

The Age of Your New Kitten

Every year thousands of kittens of all breeds and mixtures are weaned and sold or given away when they are five, six, or seven weeks old. Kittens may eat solid food as early as three or four weeks of age, although they are rarely weaned by their dam before six to eight weeks.

Many kittens that are taken from their nursery environment too soon suffer from that early separation and carry personality scars for the rest of their lives. I have known many that nursed on blankets, other animals' tails, or human fingers. Others are difficult to litter train, and some become vocal nuisances.

To avoid those problems, many cat breeders employ a safety first policy—keeping all kittens until a certain age, usually three months.

Many Bengal breeders do not release kittens until they have received one or two vaccinations. To observe the development of their conformation, colors, and coat patterns, some breeders keep their kittens until they are several months old.

I do not advocate taking kittens from their siblings and dams at an early age. Neither do I find fault with placing a particularly independent and adventuresome, strong, healthy kitten into a carefully selected new home before the

---

TIP

Parting Ways

Kittens are individuals, and the time for each to leave the nest is best judged by the breeder, who has the opportunity to watch the litter from birth.

traditional 12 weeks of age. The determining factor is its maturity, not its age. Some kittens are not ready to leave the nursery at 12 weeks.

If a very young kitten is acquired, special consideration must be given to its diet, safety, and health. That special care should be discussed both with the breeder and with your veterinarian.

Try a Mature Pet

Acquiring an older but youthful pet denies you the fun and experiences related to a frisky two- or three-month old kitten, but you will be compensated in several ways for that loss. The initial vaccination costs have already been absorbed. The time of greatest susceptibility to infectious diseases has passed. A cat acquired at six months of age will likely be more stable.

Choosing the Sex

As you begin to look at available kittens, you should consider the sex of the Bengal in your future. When you shop for a breeding queen, you will find that those available are expensive and somewhat limited in number. If a pet is desired, and you are not planning to breed your Bengal, either sex will do, the number of kittens available for your selection will be dramatically increased, and prices will reflect the increased supply.

Male kitten on the right, female on the left.

Females

Before choosing a pet Bengal, you should know something about the sexual activities of cats, so that you can make a more informed decision about which gender you prefer. Female cats have an estrus cycle of 20 to 30 days that begins at about six or seven months of age. The period of visible estrous, also known as being "in heat" or "in season," happens once every three to four weeks, and females stay in season for five to 14 days. Many indoor queens' estrous cycles continue to repeat year-round. The outward signs of a queen in heat are usually very apparent, sometimes even bizarre.

Females in season exhibit many peculiar and erratic signs, and a resolute desire to escape from the house. They rub their chins, necks, and faces on the carpet while holding their hindquarters

TIP

Obtaining a Pedigree

For a fee, The International Cat Association (TICA) will furnish either three- or five-generation pedigrees to owners of cats that are registered by that association.

---

elevated and their tails off to one side. Queens in heat may be uncommonly affectionate toward humans or other pet companions. They yowl and cry in strange voices, sometimes in the middle of the night. They often roll about on the floor with their bodies gyrating. When petted, they elevate their rear quarters in an exaggerated manner with each hand stroke along the back. Their appetites are often decreased.

Male cats of the neighborhood are attracted to your home when your queen is in season. They hear her mournful crying and set up camp outside the window, as eager to meet the queen as she is to find a mate. Sometimes more than one tom is attracted to the queen's home and the din of brawling tom cats fills the night.

If she happens to escape from her confinement and slips out of the house for a few minutes, she will probably return in a family way. If that happens, you must assume the responsibilities that accompany her pregnancy, raising and finding homes for her brood of mixed kittens. If you do not wish to face those prospects, there is a better way to care for your female Bengal pet.

Spaying (ovariohysterectomy): Spaying a young, healthy queen is a surgical procedure that is performed dozens of times a week in busy veterinary practices. Major, irreversible, abdominal surgery should not be taken lightly, but because it is an operation that is done so frequently, the techniques used are well developed and are very safe in the hands of an experienced veterinary surgeon.

The advantages to spaying your queen are many. The cat's estrous cycle no longer occurs, her personality and habits are more predictable, and she will concentrate more on her human companions. Registered spayed females can be shown in alter classes in cat shows.

Talk to your veterinarian about spaying her at an early age, and certainly before her first heat. Monetary savings will result as well as health benefits to your feline friend.

Males

If you decide upon a male Bengal pet, you can expect him to reach puberty at about six to ten months of age. Like queens, males also have a heat cycle. It begins at puberty and is continuous from that day forward until they

Kittens galore.

I can't keep this kitten business a secret much longer.

die or are castrated. At puberty, males begin to show evidence of wanting to hit the streets to pursue their reproductive instincts. They become more aggressive toward other male cats, and if other unneutered males (toms) are in the household, skirmishes will probably occur. They may remain affectionate and docile toward their human companions, females, and altered cats, but sexually mature toms are difficult to keep in a home environment.

Male cats make their presence known by spraying very foul-smelling urine on vertical surfaces, such as doors, drapes, or furniture. It is an instinctive territory marking technique peculiar to all domestic and wild cats.

If he escapes from the house, he may return bloodied, and in need of medical care from

An 8-week-old silver spotted kitten.

encounters with other neighborhood males. You must also accept responsibility for his significant contribution to the unwanted kitten population of the neighborhood. For those reasons, most people prefer to have their adult,

unneutered male pets castrated at about the time puberty is reached.

Castration (Orchiectomy): Castration can be safely accomplished anytime after your male Bengal kitten has received his vaccinations. Castrating (neutering) a male cat usually costs less than half the fee charged for spaying a female. It is a simpler procedure with fewer potential complications, and shorter anesthesia time is required. However, if he begins to show signs of wanderlust or spraying before that age, your pet can be neutered earlier. Castration is not the same as a vasectomy, and as in a spay operation, the surgery is not reversible.

The advantages of castration are many. Attitude changes may be dramatic. Neutered males are more human oriented and predictable. They lose the desire to escape from the house at every opportunity, and if they get outside, they are less likely to get into trouble. The propensity to spray urine ceases and their urine loses its rank odor. Neutered males may also be shown in classes for altered cats.

Choosing a Healthy Kitten

A great deal can be learned about the health and personality of kittens by watching a group at play. You should look for a kitten that appears bright, mischievous, and alert. Choose one that is adventuresome and friendly. Select a kitten that comes to you if possible. One that hides and remains quiet is probably not ready to leave the nest.

Kittens that sit with their heads down, disinterested in their surroundings, are probably not well. If quiet, lethargic kittens are seen in a group, ask the breeder about them. If kittens sneeze or have discharge from their noses or eyes, go home and return in another week—or choose another source for your Bengal. Do not purchase a kitten that appears unwell, no matter what guarantee is offered.

Drag a toy in front of the kittens and watch their response. Healthy, alert kittens show immediate curiosity and playfulness. When you pick a kitten up and hold it close to your body, it should feel soft and squirmy with a clean, soft coat.

Look at its eyes. They should be bright and clear, without redness or discharge. The color of the nose pad depends somewhat upon the bloodline of the Bengal, but it should always be damp and clean, without any caking or discharge from the nostrils. A healthy kitten's skin is supple and when a small section of skin over the back of the neck is gently lifted and released, it should immediately snap back. If it doesn't, the kitten may be dehydrated, an indication of disease. The membranes in its mouth should be bright pink.

Important Documentation

With your purebred Bengal, you should receive several important documents including a pedigree and registration.

Pedigree

A pedigree is not a registration document. It is a genealogical chart of your pet's ancestors, showing their names and show titles. It gains importance if you decide to show or breed your Bengal, otherwise it is only a coat of arms.

Registering Your Bengal

Registration papers will originate from whichever association registered the parents.

*Several documents should accompany
the kitten.*

Most Bengals being produced today are registered with TICA.

When the breeder registers a litter with TICA,
an *Application for Registration of a Cat of a
Registered Litter* (blue slip) is furnished to the
breeder for each kitten in the litter. The blue
slip that you receive lists the kitten's birth date,
color, sex, and eye color. You choose a name
for the kitten and put it and information about
yourself on the blue slip, and then you mail it
to TICA with a registration fee. The permanent
registration certificate is sent to you within a
few weeks. At the present time, TICA's fee for
permanent registration of a litter-registered
kitten is $10.

Show or Breeding Agreement

If you purchase a Bengal that is represented
by the breeder to be of show quality, that
should be stated in a separate signed document. Such a document should also define a
show-quality cat, and state what recourse you
have if the Bengal does not perform to the
level of the breeder's expectation. Technically,
any registered Bengal of the fourth generation
or beyond may be entered in a show, but few
will place or win in their classes.

Health and Vaccination Record

A document should be furnished that lists
the names and dates for all vaccinations
given, as well as the person's name who
administered the vaccinations. It should cite
the recommended date for booster vaccinations as well.

If your kitten was seen by a veterinarian for
any reason, the date and purpose of the visits
should be shown, as well as the name and
address of the veterinarian consulted. Results
of fecal examinations and worm treatments,
including the dates and name of the products
used, should be listed. The health and vaccination record, or a copy of it, should be given to
your veterinarian.

Dietary Information

You should receive a record of your kitten's
diet, including the type of food (canned,
semimoist, or dry), brand name, and quantity
of each kind of food that is being fed. You
may change its food, but all changes in diet
should be made gradually. It is therefore
important to know exactly what is being fed
when you take it home. If the kitten is receiv-
ing any supplements such as cottage cheese,
meat, eggs, vitamins, or minerals, they should
also be listed, together with the quantity
being fed.

BRINGING YOUR BENGAL KITTEN HOME

Cats travel well and safely in enclosed carriers, especially in fiberglass air travel models, with ventilation holes on all sides and a steel mesh safety door on the front.

Transporting Your Kitten

The kitten will travel better if you place in the carrier some familiar article of bedding. Tranquilization of a cat for the purpose of traveling is rarely necessary or advisable.

If your new Bengal is to travel by air, it will do well in the same type of fiberglass carrier. A cat in its carrier travels in a pressurized and temperature-controlled compartment on the plane. Cats are not usually allowed to travel on any public transportation unless they are confined to a carrier.

When to Bring Your Kitten Home

To begin your exciting new role as a Bengal owner, you should choose the best possible time to bring the new pet into your home. The more time you give to the kitten, the quicker it will bond and adjust to its new home and family.

A poor time to bring a new pet home is when the household routine is about to be disrupted, such as during busy holiday seasons. Try to choose a time when stability reigns.

Preferred types of carriers.

Doesn't anybody have a treat for me?

Training Your Kitten

By the time a Bengal kitten is old enough to leave its nursery, it will very likely be perfectly litter box trained. However, young kittens tend to play so hard that they may not have time to search out a litter box. Training can be reinforced by confinement for a few days in a small room with a litter box handy.

Grooming

Train your kitten to accept regular grooming as soon as the kitten arrives in your home. Use a soft cat brush and a fine-tooth cat comb. A few minutes of gentle combing and brushing should be repeated at least daily for the first few weeks.

Scratching

You should discourage your kitten from scratching furniture from the start. Training a kitten does not require corporal punishment. A stern "scat," accompanied by a clap of your hands is usually sufficient. Most kittens will quickly adapt to a scratching post that is kept near their beds. If a kitten persists in clawing

Bengal sharpening claws on an overturned carpet swatch.

furniture, you can enforce your "scat" with a squirt of water from a toy water gun.

Vocalizing

Your Bengal will talk to you. As it grows and matures mentally, vocal communication is established between pet and owner. Certain sounds will be associated with particular circumstances. Besides the usual cat sounds, Bengals have been known to emit short barks and loud guttural purring that are very curious and enjoyable.

However, if a kitten smells food and begins to rub on your leg, purr loudly, and utter a few meows, a bad habit is forming. When the kitten begins to sing for your supper, you need to act.

TIP

Begging and Food No-Nos

A cat's vocalization to gain attention or to beg for human food should be ignored and discouraged from the beginning. Don't make the mistake of feeding your Bengal human food from the kitchen counter or from the dining table. It is best to physically confine your pet to another room while people food is cooked, served, and eaten.

Toilet Training

Apartment dwelling Bengals and others that belong to homes with dogs as housemates are often taught to use the family bathroom facilities. Toilet training is usually effective but you must be patient. If the plan is successful, you won't have to tolerate the smell of used cat litter and your dog won't be raiding the litter box and eating cat feces. (Oh yes, dogs do love cat food, even if it is recycled.)

This training requires that you have a bathroom you can spare for cat use for a couple of weeks. Wait a few weeks until your kitten is well trained in using the box and uses it no matter where you put it. Move her litter box to the designated bathroom and allow her to use it there for at least a week. The next step is to open the top lid of the toilet and stretch a piece of plastic onto the underside of the seat ring. You must fasten it securely in such a manner that the Bengal's weight will be supported and be sure she can't scratch through the plastic and fall into the water below. Fill the hollow inside the ring with her favorite litter.

After a few days she will no doubt know that the litter is there within the toilet seat and you should then remove her old litter box and confine your Bengal to the bathroom. Leave her food and water while she is confined. Let her out of the room when you can be with her, but when she begins to look for her box, put her in the bathroom.

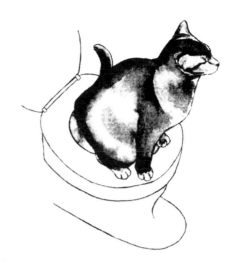

"Don't open the door when I'm busy."

Within a few days she will jump onto the toilet and use it whenever she has the urge. Then you can reduce the amount of litter daily until it is virtually empty. The next step is to remove the plastic sheet and keep your fingers crossed. A few cats never get the hang of this training and will prefer to go back to the standard litter box. A commercial kit is available that will convert a normal toilet seat to a litter box, and it can be removed when necessary for human use. The kit is complete with full instructions but the idea and its results are the same.

I think I saw a frog down there.

Getting a little crowded in there?

Suppose I should sharpen my claws on this?

One contented little family.

Now I'm getting the hang of this contraption.

Confinement

It is a good idea to confine your kitten for a short period when introduced into your home. Place the Bengal kitten's food and water dishes, its bed, a litter pan, and perhaps a scratching post in a small room. If a bathroom is used, be sure the toilet lid is kept down. Keep your kitten there continually for a few days, except when it is on your lap or in your arms. That restricted space gives the kitten a sense of security and protects it from injury while it is adapting to you.

Within a few days, after a dozen monitored excursions into the rest of the house, the Bengal will be comfortable in its new surroundings. At that time, move the food, water, and litter box to the areas you choose.

Hazards

There are many hazards around the average home. A Bengal youngster is a curious, adventuresome little creature that will get itself into trouble if not watched. A new kitten in your home should stimulate your family to identify and eliminate dangers to its health.

✔ Balls of string, yarn, or thread present major hazards to a kitten. A swallowed length of string or thread, even without a needle, can be the cause of a surgical emergency. Be sure to remove the temptations. Put sewing baskets in a closed closet or on an unattainable shelf.

✔ Insecticides and household cleaning agents represent serious dangers to the kitten (see Poisoning, page 83).

✔ Older family pets often represent some danger to a kitten during the first month, and initially a kitten should be watched carefully when with other pets.

✔ Children may not realize how delicate a kitten's body is. Bengal kittens will soon learn to evade, escape, or defend themselves from young, uninformed children. In the introductory phase of child-cat relationships, don't leave a kitten and a small child together unattended.

✔ Pet doors present a major hazard to a kitten. They may allow a kitten to get outside, and the backyard fence will probably not contain a small kitten. Car tires may screech

Insecticides present high risk to cats.

Automobiles present extreme risk to your pets.

Hazards found in most homes.

on the street in front of your home, and your Bengal may become a memory.

✔ Falling from high places is an ever present risk in Bengal homes. This risk is multiplied in apartments when cats are allowed roof or balcony access. Bengals love heights, but they can be a serious hazard to your kitten's life.

✔ Certain houseplants present dangers to cats of all ages (see Poisoning, page 83).

✔ Irons, lamps, fans, radios, toasters, and other appliances may have electric cords, which attract playful kittens.

Bengal kittens usually have an affinity for water. For a few months, it is a good idea to keep toilet lids closed. Hot tubs should be kept covered if the Bengal has access to them. A short swim might be harmless, but spas are not furnished with escape ramps for kittens.

The ultimate threat to a kitten's life is the great outdoors. Kittens that are allowed outside are at risk unless they are in your arms or on a leash. A neighborhood dog, car, bicycle, or skateboard can make short work of a kitten. Protect your pet's life and your investment. Keep your beautiful Bengal in the house!

Falling from high places is another hazard.

NUTRITION

The best and most economical way to feed your adult Bengal is to purchase small packages of an excellent or premium quality dry food.

Pet food manufacturers often do the research and formulation, providing pet owners with the analysis and list of ingredients of the foods on the supermarket shelf, so that you can make your selections based upon palatability and nutritional value for your dollar spent.

A thorough scientific study of nutritional requirements for your cat, including the interaction of enzymes, hormones, and amino acid synthesis, is presented in *Nutrient Requirements of Cats (Revised)*. The book is available to you from the National Research Council (1-800-624-6242).

Water

Water is essential to sustain life. The nonfat component of mammalian bodies is about 73 percent water. It is available from liquids and solid foods. Canned cat food, for example, is 72 to 78 percent water. Water is also supplied in smaller quantities in semimoist diets

Move over. We share, okay?

that contain 25 to 35 percent, and appreciably less in dry cat foods that are 7 to 12 percent water.

Cats will typically drink water about the same number of times a day as they eat; they are very efficient in conserving water; and they can maintain normal health in the absence of drinking water when fed high moisture diets.

Water is lost from the bodies of cats through their urine and feces. More is lost by evaporation from their respiratory tracts, mucous membranes of the eyes and mouth, and from the skin. Animals lose great amounts of water when they are suffering from digestive problems accompanied by diarrhea or vomiting. Lost water must be replaced constantly. Cats, like all intelligent beings, prefer fresh, clean drinking water.

Feeding Your Bengal

When a complete and balanced diet is offered, house cats will generally stop eating when their daily nutritional requirements are met. Bengals have mastered the art of nibbling and snacking. They will eat a dozen or more small meals a day, and will only gorge themselves if given access to large quantities of highly palatable foods.

Weigh your feline friend occasionally. Bengals are often heavier than they appear

Feeding free choice dry food is often best.

to be, due to their solid musculature and lack of soft fat.

An energetic young Bengal who climbs and exercises frequently, requires one fourth to one third more energy than one who is older and less active.

The price of cat food does not necessarily reflect the nutritional value of the product. Packaging and advertising is included in the price.

When you shop for cat food, you will usually get about what you pay for. Your Bengal's nutrition is a poor place to try to balance your household budget. House brands and generic packages may contain balanced nutrition, but their contents (and palatability) may vary.

Types of Cat Foods
The three types of prepared or formulated cat foods are: dry, semimoist, and canned. Protein digestibility ranges from 80 percent in dry cat foods, 85 percent in semimoist, and 90 percent in canned meat diets. Even though they contain meat, their formula may be only 10 percent protein, whereas a dry food with little or no animal products may contain 35 percent protein by dry weight.

Dry food: Although less energy-dense and less palatable, dry food has advantages that the other types do not share. It can be left unrefrigerated for free choice feeding. It is cleaner and easier to handle, and it usually costs less than the other two types.

Semimoist foods: These foods contain preservatives to prevent spoilage, and other elements are added to bind water. They are expensive, and feeding them frequently stimulates a significant increase in water consumption due to those chemical additives.

Canned foods: There are two varieties of canned foods: rations, which contain soy, cereal, meat, vitamins, and minerals, and gourmet foods, which contain more meat, vitamins and minerals, and less vegetable matter. Although a small rodent represents a balanced meal for a cat, a mouse is not all meat. Pure beef, pork, chicken, or fish are not balanced nutritionally. Other ingredients and supplements are included in canned formulations. Canned foods are expensive by comparison to dry foods. If the correct quantities are fed, however, spoilage is not a problem, because there should be no leftovers.

Cats have no actual fat requirement for energy. They can obtain all their energy from protein and carbohydrates. Fats add palatability to a food and some fat is needed for proper storage and metabolism of fat-soluble vitamins (A, D, E, and K). Dry foods are lowest in fat; canned foods are highest. The range is from 9 to 20 percent. Wild felines' natural diets probably contain 40 percent fat, or even more, but that does not mean that you need to add fat to the diet of your house cat.

Some owners feared the high mineral diet of cat foods caused Feline Lower Urinary Tract Disease (FLUTD), formerly known by the initials FUS, Feline Urological Syndrome. Research has shed much light on that disease, and today most high-quality cat foods contain properly balanced minerals. Several are specially formulated to maintain an acidic urine production, minimizing the risk of FLUTD. Of the three types of food available, a premium canned variety is probably the food of choice in the prevention of FLUTD (see FLUTD, page 79).

Read labels of cat foods.

Premium brands of cat foods use a fixed formula that remains constant, even when the costs of ingredients change on the market. Some other less expensive foods use a least cost formula that results in variations in the ingredients used as the prices of those ingredients fluctuate. Unfortunately, unless you contact the manufacturer, you can't be sure what type of formula is used.

Read Labels

Labels can be misleading. When reading labels, always base your analysis on the dry matter weight. Each label is a legal document. If you want detailed information about cat food labels and label terminology, you can obtain a pamphlet (for a fee) from the Association of American Feed Control Officials (AAFCO) at 1 404-656-3637.

Some labels carry the important statement: *"Provides complete and balanced nutrition for the growth and maintenance of cats as substantiated through testing in accordance with AAFCO feeding protocols."* Take special note

Atop a kitchen chair. Next stop, the tuna on the counter.

Whisker pads typical of a Bengal.

Won't anybody help a lonesome little kitten?

Is this good water or what?

of that statement. When it is seen, the product can be fed as the only source of nutrition for kittens and adult Bengals.

If you want more information about the food, such as how the analysis was made, call or write to the manufacturer. The most

TIP

Introducing Something New
Sudden changes in food often cause digestive upsets. So always add the new food to the old, in increasing amounts over a period of several days, while gradually reducing the old food.

valid analysis is obtained by animal feeding tests. That is primarily due to the fact that a laboratory analysis to establish compliance with AAFCO regulations does not necessarily address nutrient excesses, unmeasured toxic substances, or palatability.

Recipes for home-formulated diets are available in health food stores and libraries, and *Nutrient Requirements of Cats* gives some guidelines for formulating diets from natural ingredients.

Who invited you to dinner?

The age or shelf life of a product is another important consideration, especially in dry and semimoist products. After excessive storage time, some elements may be lost or rendered less nutritionally effective. For that reason, choose products that enjoy popularity among the cat owning public. For the same reason, purchase your Bengal's food from a busy store that has a high turnover of its products.

Supplements and Treats

There is no reason to supplement a Bengal's commercial, complete and balanced diet, but let's face it, you will probably treat your pet to something special once in a while. It is unlikely that your Bengal will be harmed in any way by being fed a treat occasionally. Take care not to furnish more than 20 percent of your cat's energy needs in the treats that you offer.

A better idea is to occasionally change the flavor (but not necessarily the brand) of the canned food you are using. Your feline buddy will appreciate a change now and then, and its diet will remain complete and balanced.

What Not to Feed

Table scraps: No matter how tempting, table scraps should never be substituted for cat food or used as treats. Feeding table scraps will stimulate nuisance behavior of cats when you are preparing or eating your meals. Table scraps are not complete and balanced meals for a cat. Human food seasonings and preservatives such as benzoic acid may be toxic to your cat. It is speculated that propylene glycol, used in control of water activity in some processed human foods, may be detrimental to feline red blood cells.

Special Treats
Many cats enjoy
✔ cooked eggs (never feed raw egg whites)
✔ bits of cooked chicken
✔ small amounts of cooked fish
✔ a bite of beef
If fed in small quantities, those products should cause no harm.

Raw fish: In large quantities, raw fish will cause vitamin E deficiency in cats. Commercial feline diets that contain fish are supplemented with vitamin E. Products sold for human consumption, like canned tuna, are not complete, balanced diets for cats, and should not be used as a significant part of your Bengal's diet.

Milk: Milk is dangerous to feed, even in small quantities. Adult cats are usually deficient in lactase, the enzyme that digests the lactose sugar in milk. The composition of cow's milk is significantly different from cat's milk. When fed to kittens (and many adult cats), it will frequently cause diarrhea, resulting in dehydration, reduced activity, malnourishment, and depression.

Balanced vitamin and mineral supplements: Although these may not be harmful, if you are feeding a complete and balanced diet, they are a waste of money and have no nutritional value for the cat.

Liver: Containing high levels of vitamin A, liver may cause problems in any cat, especially kittens. It is also a laxative and is a very poorly balanced food.

Candy: Why anyone would feed candy to a cat is beyond comprehension, but in case you are thinking of it, don't! Most cats have no sweet tooth, they don't need sugar or nuts, and they certainly shouldn't have cocoa, which can be toxic to cats.

The Bottom Line

Cats' palates are not as sensitive as television commercials would lead you to believe. Bengals usually prefer their food at room temperature, not straight from the refrigerator, but they are not finicky eaters. They may be fed regular meals, once, twice, or three times a day, or they can be fed free choice dry food around the clock. Kittens need at least two, and preferably three or four, meals a day if no dry food is available to them during the day.

If practical in your home, an adult Bengal may be fed free choice. In addition to the free choice dry food, offer half of a 6-ounce can of premium or excellent quality canned food each morning and evening for variety. Be sure that both the dry and canned foods contain a nutritional statement.

A 9- or 10-pound (4.1–4.5 kg) Bengal will maintain nicely on approximately 1/2 cup of dry food and one 6-ounce can of food a day, getting about half of its daily nutritional requirements from each of those two types of food. That combination should furnish about 300 k/cal. (For feeding recommendations for pregnant and lactating queens and their kittens, check with your veterinarian.

There is no reason to change brands of food periodically. It is best to find one that agrees with both your pet and your purse, and stay with it. If you decide to change brands of food, it should not interfere with the cat's nutrition, providing that the change is made gradually, and the quality is maintained.

Premium Brands

From the standpoint of the National Research Council's requirements, analysis, and compliance with AAFCO labeling, there is no particular reason for the added investment in premium foods. The increased cost of the premium diets probably can't be justified when their formulas are compared to the formulas of the excellent quality brand-name products found in grocery stores. However, when premium foods are fed regularly, you might find that your Bengal simply looks better. Perhaps a feeding trial is in order, using your Bengal as the participant.

Selecting a Brand

Try feeding a specific grocery store cat food for three or four months. Keep a record of the cost of the food, *not* the quantity eaten. Then gradually change to a specific premium food that is purchased from a pet supply store or from your veterinarian. Record the cost of the premium food eaten over an equal period of time. Note which food the Bengal preferred, and try to evaluate the cat's condition and appearance. Then make your choice accordingly.

Fat Cats

Obesity is not usually a problem with Bengals. If yours gains too much weight, stop free choice feeding and reduce its daily dietary intake by 15 or 20 percent until its weight has been reduced to the optimum. If all else fails, ask your veterinarian if your cat can profit from eating the special low-calorie, low-carbohydrate, balanced feline diet, called *Prescription Diet m/d.*

Grooming your Bengal kitten may be a chore in the beginning, but it will soon become a pleasure enjoyed by both of you.

Grooming is also one of the most important methods of communicating with your pet. It establishes a visual, vocal, and touch contact between you and your pet.

Self Grooming

Cats are great groomers. They spend hours removing dead hair from their coats with their rough tongues. They lick their feet, and with dampened toes they clean their faces and ears. Unfortunately, young kittens are likely to play, nap, eat, then play again. They don't have time for serious grooming. Their mothers took care of that task until they were weaned, and as adults, grooming will again rise to importance.

Owner's Responsibility

During the interim period, their coats still need attention, and grooming becomes your responsibility by default. Even after maturity, when their personal grooming habit is established, cats are unable to reach certain areas of

Check out these great whiskers!

their anatomy with either tongues or feet. Nearly half of their bodies, including the entire dorsum or back, is not groomed unless another cat in the household pitches in.

Cats' licking is superficial. Their tongues do not reach the depths of healthy coats and dead hair is not adequately removed. The hair that you remove from your cat with a brush and comb won't be found on your clothes and furniture. Your identity as an ailurophile (cat lover) is confirmed by cat hair on your clothes, but that is a distinction that most of us will gladly forfeit.

Small tufts or mats of dry, dead hair make the cat look unkempt and dirty. Cats often scratch at those mats, causing skin irritation, pulling out healthy hair, and leaving bare patches. Your Bengal deserves better!

Bathing Your Bengal

Bengals are usually not afraid of water, so they may be easier to bathe than some other breeds, but bathing house cats is rarely necessary. Combing and brushing usually will keep their coats clean. If the kitten takes an expedi-

TIP

Avoiding Hair Balls

Grooming the loose, dead hair from your pet's coat will also help to prevent the formation of hair balls in its stomach. They are sometimes vomited on your carpet, and although easy to clean up, they are easier to prevent. (See Hair ball [trichobezoar], page 80).

tion through fireplace ashes or some equally messy place, bathing is not difficult. First, trim its nails to preserve the skin on your hands if your pet becomes frightened. The cat should be thoroughly combed and brushed before bathing because matted hair tends to be more difficult to remove when it is wet.

A two-compartment kitchen sink is very handy for bathing your Bengal. If not available, substitute two plastic dishpans that can be set side by side in your bathtub. It will be more convenient if your sink or tub has a spray attachment. If it does not, consider purchasing a removable sprayer hose to use. Put a rubber mat or a towel in the bottom of the sinks or pans and 4 or 5 inches (10–12.7 cm) of water at body temperature of 101 to 102°F (38.3–38.9°C) in each.

Squeeze a small amount of ophthalmic ointment or sterile petrolatum ointment into both eyes to protect your Bengal's corneas. Pour a tablespoonful of high-quality feline shampoo in the first sink. Stand the cat in the side of the sink that contains the shampoo, grasping it firmly but gently by the skin over the neck, close behind the head. With the other hand, dip soapy water onto the cat with your hand and work up a lather.

Rinsing

Do not attempt to lather the face and ears. Those areas are better cleaned later with a damp washcloth. After you have thoroughly lathered the body, transfer the cat to the other sink and rinse the coat well, using the sprayer. Hold the sprayer head tight against the cat, moving it all over the body. Be sure to keep the rinse water lukewarm, neither hot nor cold. Take care not to allow the sprayer to squirt the cat in the face.

Rinse the shampoo completely from the Bengal's coat to avoid skin irritation. If no sprayer is available, rinse the Bengal by dipping and pouring water over its body with your hand or a plastic cup, or from a 1-gallon (3.8 L) jug full of warm water that you set nearby.

Drying

A Bengal's coat dries quickly. Usually a brief rubdown with a towel is all that is required. Cats usually beat a hasty retreat when they are subjected to the noise of a hair dryer, although I have known a few laid-back Persians that didn't seem to mind them at all.

Over-Grooming

How much grooming is needed? Just as a balanced, high-quality diet is necessary for a supple skin and shiny coat, an occasional bath and routine combing and brushing are equally important. However, too much of a good thing is counterproductive and you must take care not to go overboard with grooming duties. Your Bengal may resent frequent or overly ambitious grooming and no one wants each grooming session to be a wrestling match. If your Bengal formerly appreciated its grooming periods or at least tolerated them without complaining but has become less tolerant and tends to escape and hide at every opportunity, reevaluate your grooming plan.

Maybe you are combing more frequently than necessary or perhaps the sessions are too long and your Bengal has become intolerant of being held still. Perhaps the problem doesn't lie with what you are doing but is caused by some new equipment. Maybe the new brush or comb is at fault. Some cats are extremely sensitive to metal or plastic combs that have sharp or jagged teeth. Some brushes have metal or stiff, pointed, plastic bristles. Before you use a comb or brush on your Bengal, try it on yourself. If the equipment irritates your scalp, it probably is equally uncomfortable to your pet.

Bathing your Bengal frequently may remove dead coat and loose hairs and prevent your black dress or the living room sofa from looking tacky, but it may also dry the Bengal's skin and cause it to dry, scale, and itch. Like a sharp comb, too much bathing may be irritating to the pet's skin. The quality of shampoo is equally as important as a good brush and comb. Most human shampoos are not made to blend with the cat's skin pH and should not be used. Buy the best cat shampoo at a pet supply store—one that comes recommended by your veterinarian.

Dermatosis

Dermatosis is an inflammatory skin condition, which may be caused by overambitious coat care by a conscientious owner in an otherwise normal Bengal. Grooming with a poor-quality comb or brush, bathing too frequently, or using the wrong shampoo can also cause dermatosis. Whatever the cause, the cat naturally begins to lick its skin to heal the irritation but the tiny tongue papillae exacerbate the already disturbed skin and the reddened patch begins to spread. Hair is virtually licked away, and the skin oozes serum and becomes infected with opportunistic bacteria.

Veterinary aid is usually required to solve this problem and sometimes long and expensive treatment is needed. Save yourself the expense and your Bengal the discomfort. Test your grooming equipment, groom for short sessions three times a week, and bathe your pet only as frequently as needed.

How to brush your Bengal.

above left: Duck, I'm gonna spray you!

above right: I'll play ball when I have time.

I'm waiting for my hourly belly rub!

Sassy, a seal mink spotted tabby.

Begin the comb and brush exercises the day your kitten arrives in your home. Grooming need not be a lengthy procedure, especially during the first few weeks, but it should be done regularly and frequently. Take care to use the comb and brush gently, and when finished grooming, spend a few minutes playing with the kitten.

If it is obvious that daily grooming is not necessary to maintain the healthy appearance of its coat, you can change the schedule to meet the needs.

Brushing and Combing

Brush and comb the coat in the direction of its grain. That is, from head to tail, and back to belly. Begin in an insensitive area such as the back of the neck and move over the entire body, including the tail and belly. If the cat grooms itself, concentrate your efforts on those areas that it cannot reach with its tongue.

Initially you should hold your pet while grooming by gripping it from the underside of its chest, with its forelegs hanging down between your fingers. If needed, a gentle grip on the loose skin over the back of the neck may be used instead. Later, your kitten can be confined to your lap, on the floor between your legs, or on a table.

The cat comb will effectively remove the deep dead hair and will pluck out small tufts or mats if your delayed grooming schedule allows them to form. If fleas are indigenous to your area, a flea comb may be used on the cat's back and around the base of its tail to bring the flea dirt to the surface. That will help to identify the need for flea treatment. Brushing smoothes the coat after combing. Some of the rubber or soft, pliable plastic brushes on today's market do an excellent job of removing dead hair as well.

Ear Cleaning

If your kitten has a dirty face, ears, or feet, a damp washcloth may be used to sponge those areas clean. If a small quantity of ear wax is seen in the upper ear canals, it can be removed with a dry cotton swab. Do not reach deep into the ear canal with a cotton swab or any other tool. If your cat is scratching its ears and excessive, dark

Best procedure for bathing your Bengal.

wax is found, have the ears examined for ear mites with an otoscope by your veterinarian. (See Otitis externa, page 80).

Care of Toenails

Some cats do not like to have their claws cut, and they become very obstreperous when their feet are held and their claws are extended. Because scratching posts are not always the perfect answer to furniture damage, it is essential that you cut your cat's claws. Usually, the procedure takes only a couple of minutes and needs to be repeated only every two or three weeks.

Until you and your Bengal become comfortable with the procedure, claw trimming is easiest if two people handle your pet. One holds the kitten while the other manages its foot and the nail trimmer. Use a trimmer that cuts cleanly, without crushing the nail. Hold a foot in one hand, with your thumb gently pressing the top of the knuckles. As pressure is applied to a toe knuckle, the claw will extend. The claw is pink at its toe attachment, and the sharp tip is transparent. In a bright light, the blood vessels within the nail are easy to see. They are pink and extend from the toe into the nail in a tapered, curved line. Slip the nail trimmer over the sharp tip of the nail, staying well ahead of the pink vessels.

If you cut too close to the vessels, you may see a drop or two of blood. That is rarely a serious problem. Before you start to trim the nails, place a dry bar of soap and a shaving (styptic) stick where they are handy. If a drop of blood is seen, press the cut end of the bleeding nail into the dry bar of soap as if trying to scoop out some of the soap with the toenail, then hold the kitten for five

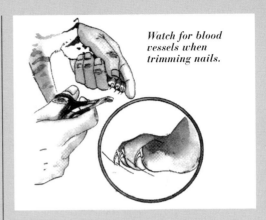

Watch for blood vessels when trimming nails.

minutes. Usually, the soap will stop the bleeding without further treatment.

If the bleeding continues, dampen the shaving stick with a few drops of water and press the dampened stick to the cut end of the nail, holding it there for a minute. Keep the kitten confined in a carrier or on your lap for 15 or 20 minutes after a bleeding nail has been treated, so that the bleeding will not start again.

Gently swab outer ear canals.

SHOWING YOUR BENGAL

All registered Bengals that have three generations of registered Bengals in their background may be shown.

Who Can Be Shown?

If you have a show cat, you are obviously interested in cat shows. Even if your registered Bengal was purchased as a pet, it can be shown if it has Stud Book status. If you believe that your pet Bengal deserves to be exhibited, and if it meets the show criteria, there is no reason not to show it. A cat show is a fun way to spend a weekend, to look at the finest specimens of your favorite breeds, and to meet other Bengal fanciers.

Pet Classes

Household Pet classes are gaining popularity year by year. There is as much excitement and competitive spirit among pet class cat owners as among established cat breeders in championship classes. In TICA shows, household pet winners receive not only ribbons and honors among their peers, they also earn titles comparable to breeding cat classes. They compete for

Master, Grand Master, Double, Triple, Quad, and Supreme Grand Master titles. In addition to ribbons and titles, the winners are given recognition in the yearbook and at the regional and international awards ceremonies.

If you aren't taking excellent care of your cat, show exhibition will probably be a disappointment. A cat in poor physical condition or one that is not well groomed has little chance of being "put up" in competition. A judge may look beyond its best qualities and only see the evidence of a poor diet or grooming.

If you plan to show your Bengal in the kitten class (four to eight months old), consider another point. Unless it is outstanding, a very young animal will rarely win against one that is three or four months older. Also remember that the period before six months of age is the most susceptible time for contracting contagious diseases. Be sure your Bengal is up to date on vaccinations!

Cat Shows

If you have not yet attended a cat show, now is the time to correct that oversight.

This beautiful two-year-old spotted male Bengal, Epitimee, belongs to Jean Mill.

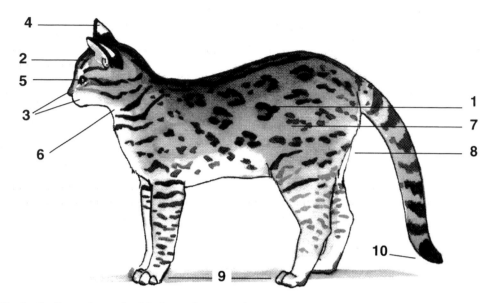

Study the Bengal standard before selecting a kitten.

1. *Coat pattern and markings: Distinct horizontally aligned or random spots in extreme contrast to background color. Rosettes very desirable. No vertical stripes. Spotted belly. Bold chin-strap and mascara markings desirable.*
2. *Bridge of nose extends above eyes.*
3. *Broad muzzle, prominent whisker pads.*
4. *Medium small ears, rounded tips.*
5. *Large, oval, wide set eyes.*
6. *Proportionately long, thick, muscular neck.*
7. *Muscular legs and torso.*
8. *Hind legs slightly longer than front.*
9. *Large, round feet.*
10. *Tail thick and tapered, round very dark tip.*

Only attending a show in person can give you the feeling of excitement that is alive in the show hall. You will discover a couple of hundred cats and their owners, cages everywhere, and at least five or six judging rings in use at the same time. To the novice, it is utter chaos, but actually, cat shows are well organized. Take a day off from your routine and go to one, if only as a spectator. Arrive early in the morning, buy a catalog, and follow an experienced exhibitor around through the maze of cages and people. Whether or not your Bengal is entered, it will be a day well spent.

TICA Bengal Standard

Only a few of the general aspects of the Bengal standard follow. A complete standard may be obtained from The International Cat Association (TICA) (see Cat Associations, page 92).

General description: The goal of the Bengal breeding program is to create a domestic cat that has physical features distinctive to the small forest-dwelling wild cats, but with the loving, dependable, temperament of the domestic cat. Keeping this goal in mind, judges shall give special merit to those characteristics in the appearance of the Bengal that are distinct from those found in other domestic cat breeds.

Conformation: The conformation gives the Bengal cat a basic feral appearance. It is medium to large, sleek, and very muscular with hindquarters slightly higher than the shoulders. The head is a broad modified wedge with rounded contours, longer than it is wide, with a large nose and prominent whisker pads. The ears are medium set, medium small, short, with a wide base and rounded tips.

Patterns: *The spotted pattern:* Spots shall be random, or aligned horizontally. Rosettes formed by a part-circle of spots around a distinctly redder center are preferable to single spotting, but not required. Contrast with ground color must be extreme, giving a distinct pattern and sharp edges. A strong, bold chin strap and mascara markings are desirable. Blotchy horizontal shoulder streaks are desirable. The belly must be spotted.

The marbled pattern: Markings, while derived from the classic tabby gene, shall be uniquely different with as little bull's-eye similarity as possible. The pattern shall, instead, be random giving the impression of marble, preferably with a horizontal flow when the cat is stretched. Vertical striped mackerel influence is also desirable. Preference should be given to cats with three or more shades; i.e., ground color, markings, and dark outlining of those markings. Contrast must be extreme, with distinct shapes and sharp edges. The belly must be spotted.

Temperament: The temperament must be unchallenging. Any sign of definite challenge shall disqualify. The cat may exhibit fear, seek to flee, or generally complain aloud, but may not threaten to harm. Bengals should be confident, alert, curious, and friendly cats.

Show Tips

Should you decide to exhibit your registered Bengal, start the procedure by telephoning the entry clerk. The name of the clerk of a nearby show can be obtained from the various Bengal associations, TICA, or the Internet. The clerk

Cats are judged individually.

Look what I won!

*A lonely Bengal awaits the
arrival of his playmate to
share the afternoon.*

*Extreme shows off his fabulous
rosettes.*

will furnish entry forms, the time and place of the show, directions to the hall, and information about the availability of litter, litter pans, and food.

A cat will not be judged if it appears ill or has congenital faults such as polydactylia (extra toes), tail faults, malocclusion of the jaws, or is unruly or pregnant. (Congenital faults are not penalized in the alter classes.) If your Bengal is soon due for vaccination boosters, have them done at least two weeks before showing. If the entry clerk advises you that rabies vaccination is required, be sure to take the rabies certificate with you.

If your grooming program is on schedule, it is probably not necessary to bathe your cat before a show. A judge can refuse to handle a cat if it is dirty, but bathing your Bengal immediately before a show may leave the coat undesirably fluffy. Clip the nails of all four feet before a show.

Wade through the show rules, and enlist the aid of an exhibitor friend when filling out your first entry form. Be especially careful that the class information you furnish is correct. The categories are sometimes confusing but they are well defined in the rules. The show may last one or two days, and your cat may be shown five or six times each day. If you decide to ask an experienced exhibitor to stand in for you on show day, be sure that person is listed on the entry form as your agent. The number of cats entered in a show is limited, so to assure your place in the exhibition hall, don't procrastinate. After you send in the entry fee with the completed entry form, you will receive a confirmation of your entry within days. Be sure to check all data on the confirmation, and if any errors are found, call the clerk.

Benching Your Bengal

Upon arrival at the show hall, a clerk will furnish your cat's entry number and assign it a cage. You will receive a catalog and other information pertinent to the show hall and the show itself. You confine your cat to its preassigned, numbered cage where it will remain for the day except when you groom it or when it is being judged in a show ring.

Certain rules and customs must be followed when outfitting your cage. Bench cages must be covered on three sides, but most handlers also cover the top. Some type of soft bedding is needed for the bottom of the cage. A towel will suffice.

Show Necessities

There are a few important items to take to the show with you. Some shows furnish litter and litter pans, but if your cat is finicky about the type of litter used, better take your own. The same applies to food and water. They may be available at the show, but there is no guarantee that your pet's favorite food will be there, or that the water will taste like your Bengal's usual supply.

Safety pins or spring clips are needed to fasten cage curtains and secure any loose joints in the cage. A small grooming table is convenient but not essential. Take a disinfectant to use on the cage, tables, and other items that may need cleaning.

Judging Categories

Several different judges work independently in perhaps six separate rings in the show hall. Each judging event is handled autonomously by the judge in that ring. Cats that are entered in the show are qualified to be judged in every ring. Each judge awards separate ribbons for each class. There are both specialty and all-breed judges. The distinctions are explained in the show rules. The categories established in cat shows are:

✔ Championship (unaltered adults, eight months old or older)
✔ Altered (adults that have been neutered or spayed)
✔ Kittens (between the ages of four and eight months)
✔ New Breed and Color or Provisional (breeds or colors that have not been accepted for championship showing)
✔ Household Pets (must also be altered)
✔ Household Pet Kittens

Exhibiting your Bengal requires patience. Eventually, your cage number will be called to a show ring for judging. When carrying your

Bengal from the benching cage to and from the ring cage, be sure to hold your pet with a firm grip, using both arms to cradle the cat close to your body. A loose cat in a show hall is very disconcerting to everyone, and is frowned upon by the officials who often get testy with the person responsible for the escapee. Once you have deposited your charge in its ring cage, given it a quick swipe with the chamois and a reassuring speech about your love (even if it doesn't win), take your seat in the audience. The rest is up to the judge.

Judging of each cat is very brief, taking only a minute or two. The judge handles the cat, compares it to the breed standard, and after seeing every cat in the class, the awards are made. Certain cats will be called back to the judging ring at a later time for the final judging of the best of each breed against each other. Be sure to pay close attention to the announcements that are made over the public-address system and on chalkboards around the hall.

The winner.

BREEDING ADVICE

Breeding your Bengal should be done for the sole purpose of improving and perpetuating the established characteristics of the breed.

The joy of breeding Bengals should not be restricted to an elite few, but you must be prepared to research the genetics involved with selection of a mate, to care for your queen during pregnancy, to assist in delivery if necessary, to properly care for the kittens, and to locate suitable homes for them.

Your responsibility to the Bengal breed and to the community does not end when a nice litter of kittens is produced. Your work has only just begun.

One of the poorest motives for breeding your Bengal queen is to make money. If that is your objective, speak to a Bengal breeder about it. You may be surprised.

Producing kittens from pet-quality females and pet-quality males is detrimental to the breed. In any breed, especially one as new as the Bengal, many pet kittens are produced by dedicated breeders who are striving to improve the breed. Even in the most carefully planned

Colour Stay's spots before your eyes.

litters, a small percentage of the kittens is of breeding or show quality.

Veterinarians often say with a wry smile that all adult queens are spayed, in season, or pregnant. That exaggeration isn't far from true. Queens begin their heat cycles between six and nine months of age and each heat period lasts one to two weeks. The queen can be bred at any time during that period, which repeats every month. That reality plus the fact that a queen in heat yowls, rolls around on the floor, tries to escape, and makes a terrible nuisance of herself should cause any owner to strongly reconsider breeding a Bengal queen.

Breeding Complexities

The most common reason stated by owners for breeding a queen is "to teach the children about the miracle of birth, and to let them watch the kittens grow." However, too often the children's parents aren't informed about cat breeding and queening procedures, required nutrition and vaccinations, and other complex-

Mother aids in delivery of kitten.

The mother begins cleaning the newborn kittens immediately.

ities of cat breeding. Add to this the complex genetics of purebred Bengal breeding, and most amateurs are flirting with disaster.

Breeding pet-quality Bengals will downgrade the breed, and this practice should never be considered. Veterinarians generally advocate the practice of stewarding pet populations because of the abundance of unwanted cats, both mixed breed and purebred. The daily euthanasia of thousands of shelter cats, and

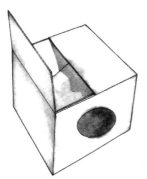

A nesting box is a very private place.

the great reservoir of infection that's propagated among feral cats are also reasons for stewardship. Bengal breeding should be left to professional breeders who are trained and have experience with the genetics and standards of the breed.

Profitability Issues

You might want to consider breeding your queen if she is show- and breeding-quality, has reached two years of age, and has been proven to be an excellent example of the breed by virtue of her show wins. However, you must remember that the profitability of raising Bengals is quite problematic.

If the above discussion doesn't dissuade your determination to raise a litter of kittens, buy a good Barron's book on cat breeding, read and digest it, and then take the proper course of action.

CHECKLIST

Breeding Bengals

This list will help answer your questions relative to breeding your Bengal queen.

✔ Check the Bengal kitten market. Talk to breeders and see what they think about raising a litter. Study all you can find about the Bengal breed. Ask show judges and owners for advice.

✔ Your female Bengal should be at least one or two years of age and hopefully been exhibited at several shows before she becomes pregnant.

✔ Read a good book about breeding and raising cats, such as *The Complete Book of Cat Breeding* by Barron's.

✔ Two to four weeks before anticipated breeding, a health and breeding exam should be performed by your veterinarian. Record his or her advice.

✔ Vaccination boosters should be updated by a veterinarian.

✔ Laboratory examination for internal parasites should be done by your veterinarian.

✔ Have your female "faulted" by an experienced and reliable Bengal breeder or a show judge.

✔ Find a healthy Bengal male that has produced healthy litters of kittens and sign a contract with his owner after you've reviewed his pedigree, his wins at shows, and his physical characteristics that improve upon your queen's shortcomings.

✔ Be sure you have adequate facilities to raise a litter of kittens, which means a quiet, easy-to-clean room, out of the traffic pattern of your home, complete with nesting or queening box.

✔ Have appropriate help available if the queen should require assistance during delivery. Get an emergency phone number for your veterinarian.

✔ Take the queen to the tom at breeding time and leave them together at least a day or two. Be sure to consult with the stud's owner about housing your queen while being bred.

✔ Pay strict attention to the care and nutrition of the pregnant queen and prepare for kittens approximately 59 to 63 days from breeding date.

✔ As the queening date nears, confine the queen to the area you have chosen for her. Don't let children handle her during this somewhat reclusive period when she is a bit moody and reluctant to receive visitors.

✔ Spend the time to find good, reliable, appreciative homes for the kittens. This doesn't mean just a newspaper ad.

HEALTH CARE

Providing health care for a Bengal is no different from that of any other breed of domestic cats. Bengals have no recognized idiosyncrasies that require special health care considerations.

The health of your cat depends upon many factors, including proper immunization. To vaccinate a kitten and provide it with food and water does not assure its good health. The health or disease status of a cat is affected by physical, emotional, infectious, and nutritional stress factors. Those factors are related to the genetics of the cat, exposure to diseases, the population density of the environment (the number of cats in the household or cattery), the quality and quantity of nutrition provided, exercise provisions, sanitation of the physical environment, and both natural and induced immunity to diseases.

Hybrid Vigor

Many hybrid animals of other species seem to enjoy a certain degree of hybrid vigor (heterosis). That term is used to describe a phenomenon wherein the offspring of parents of two different species possess a greater strength

Bengal buddies climb on a platform tree.

or resistance to disease than either parent. Bengals of the F-1 generation are reported by many owners and breeders to be extremely disease-resistant, hardy animals. Whether Bengals of the fourth generation and beyond express hybrid vigor is only conjecture.

There is reason to believe that the Asian leopard cat is resistant to feline leukemia virus (FeLV), which causes a very serious disease in domestic cats. One might speculate that some of that resistance may be inherited by domestic Bengals, but no documented proof of such resistance has been published.

Vaccinations for various diseases are important to maintain your Bengal's good health. The rapidly developing field of biotechnology introduces new immunizing agents annually.

Vaccines

Vaccines are agents that, when administered properly to a healthy animal, cause that animal to develop immunity to a disease. Some vaccines are prepared from killed bacteria, viruses, or other microscopic pathogens (disease-causing

Vaccination Schedule

A disease may be endemic in some parts of the country, and totally absent in others. That fact alone makes a general schedule nearly worthless. Your Bengal's specific vaccination schedule should originate with your local veterinarian.

organisms). Those killed products are usually considered to be safer to use, especially in very young and very old animals. They are probably inferior to the live vaccines in terms of protection because they do not replicate in the vaccinated animal's tissues and the immune response is slower and less complete.

Other vaccines are made from microscopic pathogenic organisms (primarily viruses), that have been treated in some way to modify or attenuate them. Modification allows the infectious agent to remain alive, and when it is introduced into a healthy animal it replicates in the tissues of that animal, but it is unable to cause disease. Those are modified live-virus (MLV) vaccines, and they are generally considered to confer more reliable immunity than killed-virus vaccines. Replicating vaccine viruses may be shed from the vaccinated animals (see The Bengal Vaccine Controversy, following).

Recent technical advances involve the preparation of vaccines from particles of viruses. Fragments of a virus are split away from the disease-causing organism. When administered to a healthy animal, they stimulate an immune response in the vaccinated animal, but it is impossible for the fragments to cause disease.

How a Vaccine Works

The administration of a vaccine is intended to stimulate a dynamic, ongoing process called an immune response. That response involves the production of white blood cells and antibodies that attack and destroy invading pathogens before they can cause disease. Immune response includes the establishment of a memory process (anamnesis) that hastens the response to future exposures to the infectious agent.

The level of immunity that develops from a vaccination is dependent upon the cat's health, its age, its existing passive immunity, its prior vaccination history, and past exposure to the pathogen. The degree or quality of immunity conferred by a vaccine is also related to the particular infectious agent involved, its antigenicity, the vaccine concentration, and the route of vaccine administration.

When a cat has some degree of immunity to a disease, and is subsequently vaccinated for that disease, its immunity will normally be boosted. Without boosters or exposure to the disease, its immunity gradually decreases.

A strong, healthy cat will resist disease by virtue of its good health. A healthy, active cat will respond well to vaccinations and will develop more complete immunity to disease. Vaccinations given to cats suffering from poor nutrition, disease, or other stresses may be a waste of good biologics and may give owners a false sense of security.

The Bengal Vaccine Controversy

There is an ongoing debate about the types of vaccines that should be used in Bengals. Some breeders believe that only killed-virus vaccines should be used, because the safety and effectiveness of modified-live virus (MLV) vaccines have not been proven in wild animals.

Because Bengal house pets are four or more generations removed from their wild ancestors, most health care professionals treat Bengals exactly the same as other domestic breeds. It is important to remember that Bengals are house cats, not wild animals.

There is a potential (if remote) threat that a virus contained in an MLV vaccine might revert to a disease-causing state. I have found no documentation indicating that any of the current MLV viruses have ever reverted to a virulent state and caused a disease in domestic felines.

Virus shedding may occur with MLV vaccines. The shedding is related to the fact that the MLV virus replicates in the tissues of the vaccinated animal. A shed virus is not necessarily virulent (capable of causing disease).

There are reports of virus shed from vaccinated domestic cats causing symptoms in wild cats that are housed near the vaccinated domestic cats. If you keep wild cats, your vaccination program should be discussed with health care professionals who have experience with vaccines used in those animals.

Most commonly used pet drugs and biologics have *not* been extensively researched in wild animals. The fact that a product is safe and efficacious in one species does not necessarily mean that it is dangerous or ineffective when used in other animals, but there is always a question.

A majority of the veterinary practitioners that I contacted, who have occasion to vaccinate *wild* felines, use killed vaccines when available. Those who administer MLV vaccines did not report adverse reactions to those vaccines and they trust MLV vaccines to confer

---

═══ TIP ═══

Booster Shots

It is important that booster vaccinations are given to stimulate and maintain the anamnestic (memory) response in a vaccinated animal. Vaccines are not perfect.

---

good immunity to the animals on which they are used.

The U.S. Department of Agriculture, Biologics Section, advises that there are no federal regulations that govern the use of MLV vaccines on hybrid outcrosses from the Asian leopard cat and the domestic cat. Their policy is to leave the administration of any biologic to the discretion of licensed veterinarians.

Representatives of three major companies that research, license, produce, and distribute feline vaccines were contacted. They agreed that there is no research data to support their opinions, but their products are assumed to be safe and efficacious for use in domestic Bengal cats. None were aware of any adverse reactions to their products when used in domestic Bengal cats, hybrids, or wild animals.

Many veterinarians who specialize in feline medicine use killed-virus vaccines in exotic felines such as the lynx and Asian leopard cats. Bengals are treated the same as any other domestic cat in virtually every way. If a particular vaccine or therapeutic agent is not considered efficacious or safe for use in other house cats, it will not be used in Bengals. Products used in other cats are also used in Bengals.

Vaccine-associated fibrosarcoma is a tumor formation that occurs as an aftermath to

Precious, a seal mink marble tabby.

vaccinations. It generally follows site inflammation of feline leukemia virus or rabies vaccination. A task force, cooperating with the AVMA and the AAFP, has published various recommendations to prevent occurrence of vaccine-site fibrosarcoma. Ask your veterinarian to discuss this phenomenon at the time your Bengal is vaccinated.

Infectious Diseases

Rabies: A lethal disease of all mammals, rabies is transmitted by direct contact with the saliva of an infected animal. Bats are attractive prey for Bengals. If bats exist in your area and might enter your house, be aware that many are infected with rabies. Rabies vaccination requirements vary from place to place according to local ordinances and in at least 12 states' statutes. Consult with your veterinarian about the age at which your cat should be vaccinated, as well as the need for booster vaccinations.

The most common reservoirs of infection for rabies virus are raccoons, bats, skunks, and other wild mammals. All rabies vaccines currently in use are killed-virus products.

Healthy cats may be vaccinated initially between three and six months of age, then again when a year old. A booster may be given every one to three years, depending upon the particular vaccine used and the laws that apply.

Feline leukemia virus (FeLV): This virus causes a complex, often fatal disease in cats that may be manifested in many different ways. It may suppress the cat's immune system and cause severe anemia, and it is frequently associated with cancer of the lungs and kidneys. Often, the only outwardly visible symp-

Tough job but somebody has to do it!

toms are gradual health degeneration, weight loss, lethargy, and depression.

FeLV can be contracted through bite wounds and other contact routes, or it can be transmitted from mother to kittens before or at the time of birth. Blood tests can detect FeLV, but the interpretation and significance of test results are controversial in the health care community at this time. FeLV tests and vaccination programs vary from one area of the country to another, and from year to year, as new research results are published and new biologic products are developed. Because FeLV is so unpredictable, your health care professional should be consulted before vaccinating.

Feline immunodeficiency virus (FIV): FIV is similar to but antigenically unrelated to the feline leukemia virus. It is classified as a slow virus, in the same class as the virus that causes AIDS in humans. This feline virus is highly species-specific and, according to current knowledge, it affects only cats. It is commonly spread by bite wounds and is rarely seen in house cats. Aggressive, free-roaming cats are the usual reservoir of infection. An antibody test is available to help diagnose this currently unpreventable and untreatable disease.

Feline panleukopenia virus (FPV): Also called cat distemper or feline enteritis, FPV is one of the most common and severe viral diseases of cats. It is especially lethal in young kittens, but it can cause death in cats of all ages. In the very young, there may be few identifiable symptoms. The kitten may appear normal one moment and become lethargic and limp a few hours later. Within a few more hours, the infected kitten may be comatose or even dead. In older cats, the symptoms usually include severe diarrhea, vomiting, and dehydration.

A series of vaccinations against panleukopenia is recommended for all kittens, beginning by eight to ten weeks of age, depending on the circumstances. Annual booster vaccinations are essential.

Feline viral rhinotracheitis (FVR): One of several upper respiratory diseases of cats, FVR is typically manifested by sneezing, purulent ocular and nasal discharge, and redness of the membranes of the eyes. Cats affected with this disease often dehydrate rapidly, and frequently they have no appetite. Those complications make the disease noteworthy in all ages, but especially in the young. Rhinotracheitis may be accompanied by pneumonia, which can be fatal.

FVR is spread by aerosol (sneeze) contact from infected cats. It is most prevalent in outdoor cats or in animals that come into contact with infected cats in boarding kennels or cat shows. House cats can contract the disease from infected cats through open, screened windows.

Vaccination is recommended for all cats. The vaccine is often packaged in combination with other vaccines.

Feline calici virus (FCV): This virus causes erosions on the tongue, lips, gums, nostrils, throat, and sometimes eyelid membranes. It is often complicated by a reduced appetite and dehydration. It usually runs a relatively short course, and is rarely fatal. The secondary appetite loss and dehydration problems can be very serious, and the infection reduces the animal's resistance to other diseases. It often accompanies rhinotracheitis, and is also spread by aerosol.

Vaccinations are recommended for all cats, using the same schedule as FVR and FPV vaccinations.

Feline chlamydiosis (pneumonitis): A disease that is manifested by sneezing and inflammation of the membranes of the nostrils and the eyes, feline chlamydiosis is caused by the Chlamydia organism that is neither a virus nor a bacterium. The infection produces symptoms similar to FCV and FVR. It is highly contagious and may occur in cattery situations as a neonatal disease. It is treatable and is thus less dangerous than FCV or FVR. Unfortunately, all three of those diseases may infect a cat concurrently.

Chlamydia vaccine is a killed product that is frequently combined with the vaccines for FPV, FCV, and FVR. The same vaccination schedule may be used.

Vaccines for the upper respiratory diseases discussed above are usually protective, however they are not 100 percent effective under all circumstances. Booster vaccinations are very important.

Third eyelids pulled up are a sign of illness.

Feline infectious peritonitis (FIP): A lethal viral disease of cats, FIP symptoms in the early stages include a persistent fever, but other signs are very obscure. Later, infected cats may suffer from abdominal or chest fluid production. There is no known successful treatment for the disease. It does not occur as frequently as the other feline diseases discussed, and is not as well understood as most other cat diseases.

A vaccine is available, but veterinarians often recommend FIP vaccination only in high-risk situations.

Feline lower urinary tract disease (FLUTD): In a class by itself, FLUTD claims thousands of lives of adult male cats annually. Until the advent of new, carefully balanced, commercial diets for cats, FLUTD was one of the most common, potentially fatal diseases seen in male cats.

FLUTD is a blockage of the urethra of male cats caused by mucus plugs and tiny sandlike stones (struvite crystals) that originate in the bladder. Within hours after total obstruction, the cat begins to suffer intense abdominal pain, and if not treated very early, the cat will absorb toxic waste products from his urine. Kidney degeneration and uremic poisoning follow, and the cat will die.

The mucus and crystal formation probably occurs in many female cats as well, but due to the anatomical differences between the male and female, only the male's life is frequently at risk. A male cat's urethra bends around the pelvic bone, then it narrows as it passes through the penis. Solid and semisolid particles collect in that curved funnel, and an obstruction is formed. The shorter, wider, more elastic urethra of the female allows mucus and "sand" to pass without obstructing urine flow.

FLUTD is a medical emergency! If symptoms are observed, your veterinarian should be called immediately.

Initially, an affected cat makes frequent trips to his litter pan. He strains for a few seconds, then leaves the pan, only to return a short while later and repeat the process. He licks his penis and perineal area frequently. When you check the litter to see if any urine has been passed, you may see no urine, or perhaps only a few drops, with a drop or two of blood.

As the condition progresses, he squats in the litter box in a urinating or defecating position for extended periods of time, and often cries in pain. By that time, he will be totally disinterested in food and water. Later, he will appear disoriented and glassy eyed. He will lie on his side and cry in pain when he is touched.

Cats sometimes give their owners early warning that they have urinary disease. They will jump into a sink, or onto a countertop or table, and urinate. Often the urine will contain a few drops of blood mixed with the urine. If that is observed, take the cat to your veterinarian before other symptoms develop.

FLUTD is seen in all breeds of cats in all parts of the country. It is not as common today as it was in the past, but if it should occur, your male cat's life may depend upon early detection of FLUTD symptoms and immediate veterinary treatment.

Feline lipidosis (fatty liver disease): One of the most common liver disorders of cats occurs when large deposits of fat build up in the liver. Obese cats, especially those past middle age, often develop hepatic lipidosis. If your old Bengal has been rotund and for no apparent reason its appetite fails and it begins to lose

Just waiting for some action.

weight, take it to your veterinarian immediately. A positive diagnosis can be made by blood tests and possibly a liver biopsy, and the disease can be treated if prompt diagnosis is made.

Hair ball (trichobezoar): The formation of hair balls in the stomach and intestines of cats is a common condition. As a cat grooms itself, it swallows the hair that is pulled out with its tongue. Hair is nearly indigestible, and it often forms tightly woven mats in the stomach or upper small intestine that must be passed in the feces or vomited. A cat with hair balls may have a persistent dry cough and reduced appetite shortly before vomiting a mouse-shaped hair ball. Treatment, if required, usually employs the regular use of lubricants that may be added to the cat's food.

Gingivitis: An infection of the gums, gingivitis is usually associated with dental prob-lems such as heavy tartar on your cat's teeth. The signs usually observed include bad breath and a reluctance to pick up or chew solid food. It is a condition seen primarily in middle-aged or older cats. Treatment is usually begun by cleaning the teeth and removing the tartar. In advanced cases, a tooth or several teeth may require extraction.

Otitis externa: This infection of the outer ear canal may be related to an infestation of ear mites (which are contagious), excessive wax buildup in the ear canal, or the presence of foreign material. The cat may scratch at an ear and hold it tipped downward. You may observe a foul-smelling discharge from the ear. Treatment usually includes thorough cleaning of the ear canals, and possibly the use of drops in the ear, oral antibiotics, or a combination thereof.

Wild Asian leopard cat (male).

Wounds and abscesses: Common in outdoor cats, especially in toms, abscesses are usually the result of cat fight puncture wounds that are not treated immediately or adequately. Treatment of wounds or abscesses depends upon the location and state of the infection. Prevention is easier, cheaper, and safer than treatment! Keep your Bengal in the house.

Skin Diseases

Ringworm: A contagious fungal disease of the skin that is especially prevalent in cats, ringworm is more commonly seen in cats that are under stress from overcrowding, lack of exercise, poor nutrition, or an unclean environment. In an acute, clinical infection, skin lesions are raised, inflamed, hairless circles on the skin. Subclinical ringworm is much more common, and is manifested by scaling of the skin, broken hair shafts, and only slight hair loss.

Animals with subclinical infections may act as carriers or reservoirs of infection for other cats, other household pets, and sometimes humans. It can be transmitted by handling an infected animal, then handling a susceptible animal.

Specific diagnosis is made in a clinical laboratory. Treatment varies according to the circumstances. It may be necessary to use oral medication, topical medication, medicated baths, or a combination of techniques.

Mange: A less commonly diagnosed skin disease of cats, mange may be caused by any of several skin mites including Demodex, the Notoedric mite, or Cheyletiella.

Diagnosis is made in the laboratory and treatment is managed by specific drugs applied to the skin. Mange is often related to stress factors, and some health professionals recommend vitamin therapy and nutritional improvement in addition to the prescribed therapeutic products.

Flea bite allergy: Causing intensive itching, especially in the area of the base of the tail and along the flanks, this dermatitis is an allergy to the saliva of the flea. Obviously, the diagnosis depends upon finding fleas or the excreta of fleas on the cat, and the treatment is to rid the cat of the flea infestation.

Flea soaps and flea collars are both ineffective and dangerous. Ask your veterinarian about recently introduced safe and effective topical, oral, or injectable products to prevent and destroy fleas.

Diet hypersensitivity: Not common, but occasionally seen in all animals, diet hypersensitivity symptoms are generalized pruritus

Fleas are part-time parasites of the very worst kind.

(itching) over most of the body. After ruling out more common causes of skin irritation, diet changes may be prescribed to ascertain which ingredient in the Bengal's diet is causing the problem. Fortunately, there are now foods available that make both diagnosis and treatment of allergies easier.

Internal Parasites

There are a number of internal parasites that may infest your Bengal. Some of those parasites can be passed to kittens from an infested dam at or shortly after birth. Infestations may be the result of exposure to the parasite eggs or larvae that are shed from other infested cats as well. Not all worms or other parasites are large enough to see with the naked eye, and diagnosis is made in a laboratory.

Tapeworms: Two-host parasites, tapeworms are found in cats that kill and eat certain small rodents, or in those that are infested with fleas. Either fleas or rodents may be secondary hosts for tapeworms. If cats ingest infested fleas or rodents, the adult form of the tapeworm will develop in the intestines of the cats. Tapeworms are segmented, thin, flat parasites that grow to great lengths in cats' intestinal tracts. As the worms mature, small segments drop off and may be found in infested cats' feces or stuck to the hair around their anus. Dry tapeworm segments look like tiny grains of rice. Finding those segments is diagnostic for tapeworms.

Toxoplasma coccidial infestation: Although rare, this parasite has public health significance and should be discussed with your veterinarian, whether or not it is suspected in your cat.

Isospora: Coccidia that are much more common in cats. *Isospora* may cause chronic

Life cycle of a tapeworm.

diarrhea and weight loss in young kittens, and are seen more frequently in outdoor cats.

Roundworms: Nematodes such as *Toxocara cati* have a complex life cycle in cats. They are known to infest kittens at an early age through infested mothers' milk. Skinny, inactive kittens should be suspected of being infested. Breeding queens should have a fecal examination done before they are bred to assure that they are not infested.

Hookworms (Ancylostoma): Infestations of hookworms are rare in the United States, but when they occur, they are significant because they may cause intestinal bleeding. A thin, inactive, weak or anemic appearing kitten may possibly be infested.

Diagnosis of the above and other internal parasites is usually made through microscopic examinations of the feces of your pet. A fresh fecal sample from your new Bengal should be taken to your veterinarian for laboratory examination.

usually seen in older cats and it is especially prevalent in cats that have received steroid (cortisone) therapy.

Diabetes mellitus: Another disease of older cats, this hormonal imbalance has symptoms similar to those discussed immediately above. All of the above diseases are very complex and are diagnosed only by laboratory tests.

Hormonal Imbalances

Hyperthyroidism: A hormonal imbalance that is occasionally seen in middle-aged and older cats, hyperthyroidism exhibits such symptoms as weight loss, increased appetite accompanied by voluminous stool production, restlessness, excitability, and increased shedding. It is diagnosed by laboratory blood tests.

Hyperadrenocortism: Another uncommon hormonal disease that sometimes accompanies diabetes, hyperadrenocortism displays such symptoms as a potbelly and increased water intake with concurrent increased urination. It is

Poisoning (Toxicosis)

Outdoor cats are more likely to be poisoned than indoor pets. Cats' grooming habits often get them in trouble with poisons. They lick their feet clean, no matter what they may have stepped in.

If they get an insecticide on their feet, they may be poisoned. Boric acid is only mildly toxic, causing diarrhea and excessive salivation. Rotenone is generally considered nontoxic but if ingested by a cat, it may cause lethargy. Keep cleaning and disinfecting agents out of the reach of cats.

caption above: Morning playtime:
an F2 and an F3 kitten.

caption above left: Cameo, an ALC
that belonged to Jean Mill, contributed
significant genes to the Bengal breed.

caption left: A Bengal admires
his reflection in the water.

I might get
up when
I have time.

Marble Bengal watching a bug in the grass.

This brown spotted kitten is practicing her tango steps. Now if she doesn't trip over her own feet!

I'm planning my day. First a leap to the counter then to the top of the refrigerator.

Muscular system of the feline.

Certain houseplants may poison cats. If your pet munches on your plants, consult your veterinarian about the possible dangers from the specific vegetation that your Bengal enjoys.

Human drugs such as aspirin, ibuprofens, acetaminophens, antihistamines, and some antibiotics can be dangerous when ingested by cats.

Metabolic Diseases of Older Cats

Senile cataracts: The result of aging of the lens of the eyes, cataracts rarely cause total blindness. The normally soft, gelatinous lens material becomes hardened and opaque and appears as a white or blue structure behind the iris. The cats' other senses usually remain sharp enough to compensate for the loss of visual acuity.

Osteoarthritis: This is an old cat disease that causes swelling and loss of normal function of the joints of the body. The pain resulting from

arthritis can sometimes be reduced with medication. Do not attempt home therapy. Aspirin and several other human anti-inflammatory drugs are toxic to cats unless the dosage is calculated carefully.

Deafness: Observed in a few very old cats, deafness is a degenerative condition for which there is rarely any treatment, but the patients seem oblivious to their loss of hearing. Owners and deaf house pets find ways to communicate through touch and manage quite nicely.

Kidney failure: This degenerative disease claims many lives. Aged animals compensate for a gradual loss of kidney function by drinking increasing amounts of water. When they are unable to consume and eliminate sufficient quantities of water, they become uremic. If kidney compromise is discovered early, special diets are available to reduce the stress on those organs. When your old Bengal's thirst increases, and it is observed making frequent trips to the litter box, consult your veterinarian.

Congenital Deformities

Congenital anatomical deformities of Bengals are those that are present at birth. Some are hereditary, others are possibly genetically transmitted, but not enough data is available to be sure. The few congenital physical deformities that have been reported are not unique to Bengals.

To protect the Bengal's future, students of the breed generally agree that repeated breeding of the parents of congenitally deformed offspring should be discouraged except under

Skeletal system of the feline.

exceptional and controlled research conditions. Similarly, normal appearing siblings of a congenitally deformed kitten are usually placed as pets to be altered at maturity.

Chest compression: Occasionally, a kitten with chest compression (swimmer kitten) shows up in a Bengal litter. It is not limited to Bengals, and it does not appear to be a threat to the Bengal breed. The condition is manifested by ventro-dorsal chest compression. (Its thorax is flattened between the spine and sternum.)

It is also known by the human anatomical term *Pectus excavatum,* and is generally considered to be genetically transmitted in cats. It is believed by some to be associated with nutrition of the dam, and it may be a combination of both. It is seen in varying degrees of severity.

If you acquire a kitten that you suspect has chest compression, the breeder should be notified and your veterinarian should be consulted immediately for diagnosis and prognosis.

The parents of chest compression kittens should be removed from the breeding program because the condition is assumed to be genetically transmitted until proven otherwise.

Patellar (kneecap) displacement: Another congenital deformity that has been reported in Bengals and other breeds, kneecap displacement is assumed to be genetically transmitted as well. The condition is not life-threatening, and can usually be surgically repaired, giving a normal life to the affected pet. Affected cats shouldn't be used in a breeding program.

Congenital hip dysplasia: This deformity has been diagnosed in a few breeds, including Bengals. More information on hip dysplasia is available in the canine, where it is known to be hereditary. If the same holds true in cats, affected animals should not be used for breeding.

Other congenital deformities of cats include crooked tails and crossed eyes, as well as other ocular problems. Hair and coat peculiarities, extra toes, and other physical anomalies may occur as well. Many are believed to be genetically transmitted. If you suspect that a kitten may not be entirely normal, the breeder of the kitten should be notified immediately, and if a second opinion is desired, your veterinarian should be consulted.

Giving Your Bengal a Pill

Fortunately, many feline drugs are now packaged in flavored, liquid formulations and dropper bottles, but it is sometimes necessary to give your kitten a pill. Consider the following technique.

*Brown marble Bengal resting on her pad—
her favorite spot.*

The proper way to give a pill to a Bengal.

Sorrel spotted or "Hot Orange" Bengal.

Four precious spotted Bengal kittens hiding in a tube.

When that position is reached, the lower jaw will open. Drop the pill over the top of the tongue, directly into the throat. Immediately relax your grip on your patient's head, and as you do so, dip your right index finger in the butter and wipe it on the nostrils of the patient. The cat will quickly lick its nose to clear the nostrils. In doing so, its tongue comes forward, the cat swallows, and the pill is on its way to the stomach.

Symptoms of Illnesses

Changes in their pets' attitudes, appetites, and habits alert Bengal owners to illnesses. Sometimes it is difficult for pet owners to convey those observed changes to their veterinarians in meaningful terms.

Think carefully about the duration of the symptoms that you have observed. They may be associated with some events in the pet's life. For instance, did they begin a few days after the cat was boarded, follow a change in diet, or start after it consumed a houseplant? Make notes of your observations and use them when you call your veterinarian for advice.

A number of symptoms may be present; be sure to record all that you observe. Listed below are some general symptoms, that will help you provide a useful history for your veterinarian.

✔ **Temperature elevation:** Anytime you suspect illness in your pet, take its temperature. The normal rectal temperature of a cat is between 101 and 102°F (38.3–38.9°C).

First, put about one-half teaspoonful of butter or margarine in a saucer, near the pill, on a countertop. Wrap your Bengal in a large towel, with only its head protruding from the towel cocoon. Place your left hand (assuming that you are right-handed), palm down on top of the cat's head. Then grip its head with the tip of your thumb on the right cheek, and your index or middle finger on the left. Press the tips of your finger and thumb inward, forcing the cat's upper lips between its upper and lower rear molar teeth. As you squeeze the lips inward, tip the cat's head back, so that its nose points toward the ceiling, over its back.

✔ **Not walking:** Can't get up? Tries to rise, falls? Difficulty walking? Staggering? Lame on one leg?

✔ **Swelling:** Where and how big? Tender when touched? Scab on it? Drainage from it?

✔ **Loss of appetite:** No interest? Eats one food, not another? Refuses all food? Tries to eat, can't? Salivates when eating?

✔ **Urinary difficulty:** Strains in box? Passes no urine? Urinates in strange places? Bloody, dark brown? Foul odor? Large quantities? Sprays urine?

✔ **Water intake:** Great quantities? Drinking no water? Drinks then vomits?

✔ **Defecation:** Constipated? Diarrhea? Loss of control? Color of feces? Feces brittle or hard? Foreign material? Blood or mucus? Cries when defecating?

✔ **Vomiting:** What is vomited—Parasites? Food? Mucus? Hair mats? When does it occur? How frequently? Follow coughing?

✔ **Respiration:** Relaxed, smooth? Labored and deep? Raspy sounds? Panting? Sneezing? Coughing?

✔ **Mucous membrane color:** Gums pale, white? Gums dark red? Blue-tinged?

✔ **Skin condition:** Hairless patches? Red, inflamed? Itchy? Hair brittle? Dry? General thinning? Scabs? Blood oozing?

✔ **Attitude:** Grouchy? Super-affectionate? Hides from family? Sits instead of standing?

✔ **Eyes:** Pupils seem dilated? Pinpoint pupils? Discharge from eyes? Membranes red? Watery, squinting?

✔ **Weight and Condition:** Weight loss or gain? Obese or very thin?

Don't attempt to diagnose and treat your Bengal based on the numerous illnesses and their symptoms that have been discussed. This information is important for you to be aware of various cat diseases and their symptoms to enable you to convey your observations to your Bengal's veterinarian.

Euthanasia

It is normal for pet owners to refuse to entertain thoughts of the inevitable loss of their pets. Your new Bengal kitten will live for many years, but eventually the end will come. Hopefully it will be quick and painless for both pet and owner. In certain prolonged disease conditions, such as inoperable cancer that does not respond to therapy, you may consider euthanasia. Life and death decisions must be made by owners with the guidance of animal health care professionals. Performing euthanasia is a role that veterinarians abhor, but generally they accept the responsibility. In the caring hands of a professional, euthanasia is a quiet, painless, and comfortable way to end a cherished pet's life.

INFORMATION

Internet sites are plentiful for Bengal cats. Please remember that all information that appears on the Internet isn't necessarily factual. The Internet is an excellent place to find and reach fanciers, but the best method of obtaining knowledge about Bengals is from proven sources. Before you buy a kitten, visit the Bengal breeder, handle the dam, sire, and siblings, and study their pedigree.

Cat Associations

The International Cat Association Inc. (TICA)
P.O. Box 2684
Harlingen, Texas 78551
(956) 428-8046
www.tica.org
E-mail: ticaeo@xanadu2.net

Cat Fanciers Federation (CFF)
P.O. Box 661
Gratis, Ohio 45330
(937) 787-9009
www.cffinc.org

American Cat Fanciers Association
P.O. Box 1949
Nixa, Missouri 65714-1949
(417) 725-1530
www.acfacat.com

The Cat Fanciers' Association Inc.
P.O. Box 1005
Manasquan, New Jersey 08736-0805
(732) 528-9797
www.cfainc.org

Canadian Cat Association
289 Rutherford Road South, Unit 18
Brampton, Ontario, Canada L6W 3R9
(905) 459-4023
www.cca-afc.com

The International Bengal Cat Society (TIBCS)
121 Buhman Road
Washougal, Washington 98671
www.bengalcat.com
E-mail: secretary@bengalcat.com

Authentic Bengal Cat League
25708 E. Alsea Hwy
Alsea, Oregon 97324
www.blast.net/abcclub

Cat Magazines

An ever-changing abundance of periodicals carry information about Bengal cats, including cat shows and recent class winners. Some feline periodicals are found in major bookstores and newsstands. Names and addresses of other magazines may be found on the Internet by typing in the search space "Cat magazines."

This is as high as I can get unless I can make it to the top of the fridge.

About the Author

Dan Rice is a retired veterinary practitioner from Colorado who continues to use his knowledge and experience to improve the relationship between pets and their owners. His greatest joy is seeing well-adjusted, healthy pets in happy homes, and he recognizes that association depends upon owner information and understanding as well as pet health. To date, he has 15 published books on pets and has written several fiction works and an anthology of experiences.

Photo Credits

Anne Bartoli: page 84 (bottom); Gerry Bucsis & Barbara Somerville: pages 8 (bottom), 9 (bottom), 12, 16, 20, 24 (top r, bottom), 25 (all 3), 33 (top), 36, 40 (all 3), 41 (top, bottom), 44, 48 (top, bottom l), 49 (top, bottom), 52, 56 (all 3), 57, 64 (top), 68, 77, 81; Charles Cangialosi: pages 65, 80; Kent & Donna Dannen: page 88 (top l); Tara Darling: page 48 (bottom r); Isabelle Francais: pages 3, 4, 8 (top), 33 (bottom), 93; Leslie Hall: page 84 (top r); Jean Mill: pages 60, 64 (bottom), 84 (top l); Marta & Robert Peck: pages 21, 53, 84 (middle), 85 (top); Joy Peel: page 5; Judith Strom: pages 9 (top l, top r), 24 (top l), 28, 32, 72, 76; Holly Webber: pages 13, 17, 29, 37, 45, 61, 69, 73, 85 (bottom l, bottom r), 88 (top r & bottom), 89

Cover Photos

Front, back: Gerry Bucsis & Barbara Somerville; Inside front: Isabelle Francais; Inside back: Tara Darling

Important Note

When you handle cats, you may sometimes get scratched or bitten. If this happens, have a doctor treat the injuries immediately.

Make sure your cat receives all the necessary shots and dewormings, otherwise serious danger to the animal and to human health may arise. A few diseases and parasites can be communicated to humans. If your cat shows any signs of illness, you should definitely consult a veterinarian. If you are worried about your own health, see your doctor and tell him or her that you have cats.

Some people have allergic reactions to cats. If you think you might be allergic, see your doctor before you get a cat.

It is possible for a cat to cause damage to someone else's property and even to cause accidents. For your own protection you should make sure your insurance covers such eventualities, and you should definitely have liability insurance.

Acknowledgments

The important Bengal historical information contained in this book was made possible by the generous assistance received from Jean Sugden Mill. It is with sincere appreciation that I dedicate this book to my friend Jean.

Breeders and owners across the nation answered my plea for information, and I am also indebted to Gene Johnson, Joy Peel, Terri Pattison, Leslie Hall, Karin Donoyan, Jane Lee, Barbara Andrews, and others.

Highlights of the Bengal breed standard appear on page 62. For a complete description contact The International Cat Association (TICA), whose address appears on page 92.

All inquiries should be addressed to:
Barron's Educational Series, Inc.
250 Wireless Boulevard
Hauppauge, NY 11788
www.barronseduc.com

ISBN-13: 978-0-7641-2862-2
ISBN-10: 0-7641-2862-0

Library of Congress Catalog Card No. 2004043774

Library of Congress Cataloging-in-Publication Data
Rice, Dan, 1933–
    Bengal cats / Dan Rice.—2nd ed.
        p. cm. — (A Complete pet owner's manual)
    Includes bibliographical references and index.
    ISBN-13: 978-0-7641-2862-2
    ISBN-10: 0-7641-2862-0
    1. Bengal cat. I. Title. II. Series.

SF449.B45R5349 2004
636.8'22—dc22   2004043774

Printed in China
9 8 7 6 5